LITTLE GIANT
ENCYCLOPEDIA
OF
Proverbs

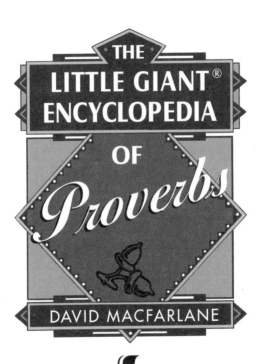

THE
LITTLE GIANT® ENCYCLOPEDIA
OF
Proverbs

DAVID MACFARLANE

Sterling Publishing Co., Inc. New York
A Sterling/Chapelle Book

Compiled by: David Macfarlane
Book Design: Karmen Quinney & Kimberly Maw

The author has strived to be as accurate as possible with the exact wording
of proverbs and with the attribution to original sources listed in the back of
the book. Our apology in advance for any misrepresentation or inaccuracy
due to the reprinting of sources.

Library of Congress Cataloging-in-Publication Data
The little giant encyclopedia of proverbs / compiled by David Macfarlane.
    p. cm.
  "A Sterling/Chapelle book."
  Includes bibliographical references and index.
  ISBN 0-8069-7489-3
   1. Proverbs I. Macfarlane, David.

  PN6405 .L57 2001
  398.9—dc19   00-067060
10 9 8 7 6 5 4 3 2 1

Published by Sterling Publishing Company, Inc.
387 Park Avenue South, New York, NY 10016
© 2001 by David Macfarlane
Distributed in Canada by Sterling Publishing
℅ Canadian Manda Group, One Atlantic Avenue, Suite 105
Toronto, Ontario, Canada M6K 3E7
Distributed in Great Britain and Europe by Cassell PLC
Wellington House, 125 Strand, London WC2R 0BB, England
Distributed in Australia by Capricorn Link (Australia) Pty Ltd.
P.O. Box 6651, Baulkham Hills, Business Centre, NSW 2153, Australia
Manufactured in Canada
All Rights Reserved

Sterling ISBN 0-8069-7489-3

Contents

Introduction

On the surface, proverbs appear to be nothing more than quaint, often pithy sayings which convey some meaning about a culture or nation—truisms which are of questionable value as a means of insight into another culture.

In actuality, it is because proverbs are often wrapped in myth that they are of value to cultural anthropologists, historians, linguists, and other social scientists. While the history of any group of individuals starts to blend with myth and superstition over a period of time, proverbs offer an indication of how a nation, culture, or ethnic or linguistic group sees itself regardless of historical accuracy.

The sources of proverbial wisdom can be pretty much anything. For the Hebrew people, a large portion of holy scripture has been recorded as proverbs. Among any group of people, the recorded statements of their most prominent members evolve into both proverbs and lore over a period of time. A particularly troubled or oppressive history offers fertile ground for the creation of new proverbs—the impact of the Holocaust on the Jews, slavery on Africans, colonialism on Latin Americans and Indians, and westward expansion on Native Americans are only the most prominent examples.

In short, proverbs are the manner by which cultures and nations pass along wisdom, insight, and inspiration from generation to generation.

They act both as beacons to the young and cultural tools for leaders. Certain proverbs can be found in virtually every modern culture. Is this the result of the commonality of human existence, or just the proliferation of global culture and communication? Perhaps both are contributors to varying degrees.

Almost anywhere in the world we find some mention of the negative repercussions of "spitting into the wind." Virtually every culture recognizes that a man with one eye has a dominant position in the land of the blind. Whether or not these and other proverbs are ubiquitous as a result of common threads in human history is an issue for anthropologists to study. In the context of the book, we will assume that all humans are cousins under the skin.

The challenge is to recognize common traits, while respecting cultural peculiarities and unique qualities. The purpose of this book is to educate the reader about diverse cultures, provide some insight into far-flung places, and elicit a few laughs along the way. That the world is effectively divided into disparate nations, tribes, ethnic groups, races, and religions that often clash with one another is a foregone conclusion. Hopefully, any effort at bridging these gaps between people is enlightening, and is received in the spirit with which it is intended.

Although an effort has been made to include proverbs from each geographical region or continent of the world, the astute reader will recognize that many peoples and regions have no voice. The reasons for this are quite simple. First, proverbs proliferate in all cultures and nations to such a degree that any effort to include all or even most would result in a massive book. Second, the proverbial wisdom of some nations and cultures is not as readily available as that from other more modern areas. Ultimately, proverbs were selected because they seemed to have something unique to say about the group they represent.

This book is divided into general subheads which organize the proverbs according to what each is primarily addressing.

What are you supposed to do with all these proverbs? That is really up to you. Read them for amusement and edification. Research them and find just the right one to use in a speech or address. Search out the two or three that you need as daily inspiration. Regardless of your purposes, the hope is that you will find something within this collection that is amusing, inspirational, enlightening, or simply entertaining. Proverbs have the power to be any or all of these.

About the Proverbs

African

It is generally considered an immutable truth among historians and social scientists that Africa as we know it now is the result of arbitrary lines having been drawn by "imperialist powers," who occupied the continent, subjected its inhabitants to miserable lives as slaves, and took whatever riches and resources they wanted or needed back to the homeland. Arguably, the greatest injustice in the history of humankind is that which was visited upon the African continent by these powers.

While the purpose of this volume is clearly not to revisit unpleasant parts of our collective history, it is not possible to compile a broad representation of the proverbs of Africa without acknowledging that many of these words of wisdom now spring from parts of the world to which the children of Africa were relocated as a result of the slave trade. The culture of the United States is, quite obviously, only one nation which was made much more diverse as a result of slavery. Another region of the world which has been greatly impacted by the forced exodus from Africa is the Caribbean; and as such, the reader will find a number of proverbs from Jamaica and a few from other island nations in the compilation that follows.

The boundaries of the African nations effectively mask the fact that the formation of modern states forced the members of thousands of tribes to live under individual government organizations. Arguably, Africa is still divided as much into ancient tribes as nations.

African American

It will be clear to the reader that many of the proverbs come from the time of slavery in the United States. They represent both an experience born of hardship and an earthy wisdom that is candid and often humorous.

Whatever else they may be, the proverbs in many ways represent the perspective of individuals who have arrived at a point where there is no more at stake in life than family and life itself.

American

While it is never fair to try and reduce a culture to only a few traits, it can be said that there are common threads which identify and, at least in part, define a nation and people. This is the product of a common history and common goals.

For Americans, the product of comparatively little national experience by European and Asian standards, that history has been defined by constant expansion and unbounded optimism. Periods of self-doubt have never been the result of foreign invaders. Successes have been many and failures relatively few. Americans believe that they succeed because they can.

Of course this experience is reflected in American proverbs. But do not look only for optimism and vision in the proverbs. Notice also the energy, individuality, and efficiency. This is the direct result of the immigrant experience—of a nation of people who fled one land in search of the freedom to pursue a chosen life.

Thus, a diversity is reflected in these proverbs which one should expect from a nation of foreigners. Notice each and try to determine from whence it comes. Puritan, industrialist, republican, homesteader, farmer—all were there in the beginning.

Arabic

In all cultures there is a clash between the old and the young—between experience and perception, continuity and change—that is commonly called a "generation gap." This gap is arguably more pronounced in those cultures that seek to maintain traditional heritage and practices while participating in the the modern world.

Nowhere is this conflict between the traditional and the modern more pronounced than in the Arab world. Especially evident in Iran since the revolution of 1979, but not completely absent anywhere, the differing views of young and old become most readily apparent in discussions about perceived views of the West, particularly the United States. Many Muslim clerics and older Arabs still see the U.S. as the "Great Satan," while their younger counterparts see hope and opportunity in the West and have a love for that ubiquitous export, American culture.

Proverbs are such a small thing and would seem inadequate for crossing a chasm of misunderstanding and divergent perspective, yet they demonstrate that for the most part, the act of living is the same for everyone.

Central & South American

As the second-most spoken language in the United States, Spanish provides perhaps the only opportunity for Americans to actually become familiar with foreign proverbs in their native tongue and to really practice a language through proverbs. However, do not assume that any proverb you practice on your Spanish-speaking friends will be completely familiar to them. There is a lot of space between Mexico and Tierra del Fuego, and the countries often share only language in common.

In truth, most of Latin America shares the common heritage of colonialism, which is why, with the exception of Brazil and Belize, they all speak Spanish. But for the most part, the general similarities end there. Some nations have for centuries struggled to combine the Native

American cultures with the descendants of the Spanish conquistadors. The experiment has not always gone well, unfortunately.

While the proverbs from Central and South America lack some of the more unique qualities of Hebrew wisdom and the abstract perspective of the Japanese and Chinese, they demonstrate a real commonsensical wisdom developed over centuries of struggling for survival and eking out an existence.

Chinese

If there were only one nation with which one could associate proverbial wisdom, it would have to be China. Though modern China was born as recently as 1949, following the defeat of the Nationalists by Chairman Mao and his Communist followers, Chinese culture and traditions are centuries old.

By way of extention, if China is the capital of proverbial traditions, then Confucius is the single individual with whom most people would connect the metaphoric and idiomatic expressions of experience that are proverbs.

In truth, China and Confucius have no corner on the market for proverbs. Yet one cannot deny that the longevity of the Chinese culture has not only created a scenario in which traditions are treasured and maintained, but also one in which these traditions can be viewed outside the physical boundaries of China itself as a result of the pervasiveness of Sino culture. The Confucian traditions established in China are also very much alive in Korea, Japan, Vietnam, and to a lesser extent in other Asian nations.

Thus, as a result of the myriad factors which have gone into the creation and preservation of Chinese proverbs, they are treasured and often emulated by cultures the world over. It is not at all unusual to hear Chinese wisdom used as a reference point in American culture, in part because the United States is such a mixture of different peoples, but also because Chinese proverbs are recognized globally as particularly insightful.

Because China has enjoyed and endured a history that is varied and decidedly mixed in what it has done to and for the Chinese people, Chinese proverbs occupy the entire spectrum of potential topics. The Chinese have, during certain periods, enjoyed astounding dominance and reaped the benefits of a culture that deserves credit for the invention of paper, noodles, fireworks, and numerous other items that we enjoy today. China has ruled and been ruled, fought tremendously bloody battles, and experienced most of that which is available to cultures that remain intact. As a result, Chinese proverbs can address any number of topics and scenarios.

English

Over the last several centuries the English have seen the best of both worlds. Once residents of a great empire, the twentieth-century English have seen their domain shrink in the modern era to the British Isles and not much more.

An unbroken and lengthy history as one nation has given the English the opportunity to see both good and bad, and it is reflected in their proverbs. There is a sense of humor that is uniquely British, and it exists within an attitude that is dour yet defiant, pessimistic yet satisfied enough with life.

Though they share the same language, Americans and English have not shared the same history and experience. Britain saw the brutality of the World Wars on its very doorstep, while America enjoyed the luxury of a more distant view. The British have watched an empire decay, while the American influence spans the globe. This is the result of time and experience, and eventually all empires become subject to both. Yet the English remain and flourish in the twenty-first century on the strength of a stiff upper lip and a rigid spine. While proverbs that result from a mixed history lack the unapologetic optimism of those from a younger nation, they more than make up for it in curmudgeonly character and wisdom. It is the difference between taking advice on life from a young man versus an older one; optimism simply cannot compensate for real world experience.

Hebrew

Of course, as was discussed in the introduction to this volume, proverbs are all about establishing the culture of a particular group. And it is important to note that culture includes the history, norms, customs, myths, beliefs, and practices of any group of people.

Having said that, it should come as no surprise that Hebrew proverbs tend to focus on religion, righteousness, and sin. After all, these characterisitics are inherent in religion; they cannot be separated from it. But while the proverbs associated with any religion might focus on these same facets, there is a depth to Jewish proverbs that goes beyond the intertwining of life and religion—life has been a bit harder on the Jews than the members of other faiths.

As a result of the mammoth struggles with which the Jewish peoples have been afflicted, the proverbs which originate from within the Hebrew faith incorporate the oppression and open aggression of which the Exodus and the Holocaust are only two examples. Among the great mass of proverbs that comes from nations and peoples around the world, these factors make those from the Jewish peoples unique.

Almost all of the translations which follow the Jewish proverbs are in Hebrew, but a few are in Yiddish or Aramaic and have been attributed to those languages.

Irish

Obvious reasons for the influence of the English language in Ireland are its proximity to England and the centuries that the Irish have spent as subjects of the British Empire. Throughout most of its history up to an ongoing economic boom, Ireland has been a predominantly traditional and rural Gaelic society. What you will find in this collection are proverbs that reflect images of the Irish countryside—of a commitment to small communities, farms, and families—and are indicative of a sometimes feudal existence which thankfully has passed.

Irish proverbs will, in all likelihood, bear some resemblance to those of England and perhaps other Western European nations. More interesting will be commonalities between Ireland and, say, Japan or the Arab world. This will truly reflect not a common cultural life spring but rather a pattern of shared experience which is the thread that binds all human life.

When available, the original Gaelic transliteration of the Irish proverb has been included.

Italian

Italian proverbs are those of a European nation with an extensive history. It becomes difficult to discern from where a number of them originated, and many of the same proverbs appear in books of Italian. Just in case you'd like to learn Italian and dazzle a loved one, we have included the Italian translation of each proverb.

Japanese

While there is undoubtedly a common thread to proverbs from all corners of the globe, one can also discern a great deal about an individual nation by analyzing the proverbs which emerge from that respective culture. In Japan, proverbs are called *kotowaza* and are quite often derived from the natural world. Many Japanese proverbs, as well as much of the Japanese culture, are the children of ancient China. But of course, as Japan has modernized and opened itself up to the world over the last century, axioms and sayings from the West have crept into everyday Japanese.

Mexican

Though we may be completely aware of what proverbs say about a nation and people, we may not always be aware of the derivation of all of the proverbs that survive to be passed down from generation to generation. In actuality, proverbs travel in the same manner as do people. When one nation conquers and occupies another, an indelible mark is left.

Mexico is an excellent example of the progression of proverbial wisdom. There can be no doubt that proverbs in Mexico today descend directly from the conquering Spanish empire. How do we know this? Well, for starters, Spanish was not spoken in the new world before the arrival of the Spanish, so some, though not all, of the myths and tales in Latin America today must descend from the Spanish. A larger question is how much of Mexican proverbial wisdom might have come from the Aztec empire, which the Spanish destroyed upon arrival.

Of course, that may be the primary concern of anthropologists only. From our perspective, Mexican proverbs are imbued with a strong sense of community, an emphasis on strong character and values, and an obvious recognition of the differences between rich and poor. All are indicative of Mexican culture as it stands today— resilient, heavily influenced by the legacy of the

Catholic church, and layered in the complex and competing influences of disparate cultures.

Native American

Living in a particular culture, be it a small community or a large nation, most human beings find it virtually impossible to escape the influences of stereotype. In the United States, with a population that has very few opportunities to interact with Native American individuals, our perspectives are largely influenced by the media. Western movies from a bygone era romanticize the savage nature of "Indians" in opposition to heroic cowboys. Modern media attempts to recreate an accurate picture of life on the "rez."

The unfortunate result of these competing portrayals of Native American life, both past and present, is that they obscure the reality of what Native American life was prior to the forced evacuation of their ancestral lands, and is since they have been "relocated" to various plots for which the government can find no other use.

Proverbs offer a means of gaining insight into Native American community and values. As such, pay particular attention to the subheadings in this collection which contain proverbs relating to Children, Deity, and Nature. These in particular paint a portrait of a people that was and is tremendously community oriented, deeply spiritual, and as respectful of the natural world as any this earth has known. It is a perspective and portrayal of Native Americans we cannot find in the early Western films.

Russian

One cannot look back through history and say that being Russian has been easy. The brutality of the czars, two world wars in which Russia suffered more causalities than any other nation, and the murderous regime of Stalin have all had their effects.

Russians have developed a very thick skin over the years. All of this hardship has created a people that is deeply cynical and not easily frightened, and about as resilient as they could possibly be. The Russian attitude is summed up by the proverb, "One can even get used to living in Hell." This phrase must be born of the collective Russian experience.

Scottish

The reader who has been born and raised in the United States might make the understandable error of lumping together all the nations located within the British Isles. Indeed, it is probably a mistake most Europeans would expect us Americans to make.

Yet we do respective nationalities a bit of an injustice by not recognizing differences, regardless of how geographically close nations may be located to one another. The Scottish differ significantly from the English and the Irish, if only because they see themselves as distinct and unique. The Scottish also possess a cynical wit regarding death, marriage, family, and drinking that is remarkable because it is so aware of the realities of each.

It would be a mistake to portray the Scottish as negative or dour. Exhibiting a probing wit, particularly philosophical regarding alcohol, and cognizant of the qualities which make up the national character, Scottish proverbs are the equivalent of the curmudgeon who makes others laugh while also making them a bit uncomfortable.

There is, after all, something troubling about the combination of humor with insightful truth.

Encyclopedia of Proverbs

Ability

If you cannot dance, you will say the drumming is poor.
— Jamaican

He who is unable to dance says that the yard is stoney.
— Kikuyu

If man can't dance, him say de music no good.
— Jamaican

You can' prevent bud from fly over you head, but you can prevent him mek nes' in you head.
— Jamaican

Not even an angel can fulfill two missions at once.
Ain malach echad oseh shtai shleechot. — Irish

You already possess everything necessary to
become great.   — Crow

The greatest and rarest talent is to love everything
good.
*Hakisharon hagadol v'hanadeer b'yoter—le'ehov kol
davar tov.*   — Hebrew

A man's intelligence is located in the tip of the pen.
Sechel ha'eesh hu tachat chudo shel ha'et.
                                           — Hebrew

The nations of the world wish to irritate the Lord,
but they can't. What do they do? They vex Israel
instead.
*Ha'umot ba'ot l'hitgarot im hakadosh baruch hu,
v'ain yecholeen. Ma oseem? Mitgareem b'yisrael.*
                                           — Hebrew

45

If a man is to do something more than human, he must have more than human power.

— Tribe Unknown

A man must make his own arrows.

— Winnebago

Stretch your legs according to the length of your kilim.

— Arabic

A half-learned physician is a danger to life, and a half-learned mullah is a danger to faith.

— Arabic

The bride does not know how to dance and says, "The room is crooked."

— Arabic

If destiny does not fit you, fit yourself to destiny.

— Arabic

You cannot jump higher than your head.

— Russian

You cannot make a soft bed for everyone.

— Russian

The elbow is near, but try and bite it.

— Russian

Many can pack the cards that cannot play.

— English

Ability is the poor man's wealth.   — American

Acceptance

The mosque's door is not shut to he who does
not pray.
                                              — Arabic

The stone which cannot be lifted should be
kissed.
                                              — Arabic

If you don't want to be disgraced, do as others do.
                                              — Arabic

Do as most men do and men will speak well
of thee.
                                              — English

Accommodation

Give your host a little something when you leave;
little presents are little courtesies and never offend.
                                              — Seneca

When there is true hospitality, not many words
are needed.   — Arapaho

Always assume your guest is tired, cold, and
hungry, and act accordingly.   — Navajo

Action

When the snake is in the house one need not
discuss the matter at length.   — Ewe

A new thing does not come to she who sits, but to
she who travels.   — Shona

Efforts and capabilities are not the same.
                                       — Maasai

The bird will not fly into your arrow.
                                       — Ovambo

Laziness likes to justify itself for not doing anything because it cannot do everything.
Ha'atzlut ohevet l'hitztadek sh'aina osa clum mipnai sh'ain b'yicholta la'asot et hakol. — Hebrew

He who loiters hears ill spoken of himself.
— Mexican

Through faith man experiences the meaning of the world; through action he is to give it meaning.
— Hebrew

Whoever can protest against a wrong, and does not, will be punished.
Kol mee sheyesh b'yado limchot v'aino mocheh, ne'enash alav. — Hebrew

If you receive pay, you cannot sit idle, and if you sit idle, you cannot receive pay. — Hebrew

An ant on the move does more than a dozing ox.
*Más hace una hormiga andando que un buey
echado.*   — Mexican

He who assists everybody assists nobody.
                                            — Mexican

Don't do today what you can put off until
tomorrow.
Ho hagas hoy lo que puedas hacer mañana.
                                            — Mexican

Where there's a will there's a way.
Querer es poder.   — Mexican

There's no life as tiring as one of doing nothing.
*No hay vida más cansada que el eterno no hacer
nada.*   — Mexican

One man driven by distress does as much
as thirty.   — Mexican

The lazy man is apt to be envious.   — Omaha

Love yourself; get outside yourself and take action.
Focus on the solution; be at peace.   — Sioux

Strive to be a person who is never absent from an
important act.   — Osage

Deeds speak louder than words.   — Assiniboine

By asking, you can go to Mecca.   — Arabic

He is the pea of every soup.   — Arabic

A handkerchief is not tied to a head which does
not ache.   — Arabic

When you are in doubt, don't fast.　　— Arabic

The beard and the scissors are both in your hands.
　　　　　　　　　　　　　　　— Arabic

A gaun fit's aye getting, were it but a thorn or a
broken tae.　　　　　　　　— Scottish

It is weel said but wha' will bell the cat?
　　　　　　　　　　　　　　— Scottish

It's by the mouth o' the cow that the milk comes.
　　　　　　　　　　　　　　— Scottish

If a' your hums and haws were hams and haggises,
the parish needna fear a dearth.　　— Scottish

A man o' words, but no o' deeds, is like a garden
fu' o' weeds.　　　　　　　— Scottish

I carena whether the fire gae abot the roast, or the roast gae abot the fire, if the meat be ready.

— Scottish

When in doubt, do nought.   — English

The shortest answer is doing.   — English

When in motion, to push on is easy.   — English

Action without thought is like shooting without aim.   — American

Bad actions lead to worse reactions.

— American

In great action, men show themselves as they ought to be, in small action as they are.

— American

Adaptation

One can even get used to living in Hell.

— Russian

The world hasn't shrunk to a wedge.

— Russian

Wheat stalks heavy with grain learn how to bow their heads.   — Chinese

Admiration

The great wall stands; the builder is gone.

— Chinese

No matter how tall the mountain, it cannot block out the sun.   — Chinese

A full bottle makes no sound; a half-full bottle sloshes around. — Chinese

One whose breath is felt in heaven. — Chinese

No man is a hero to his woman. — Swahili

When the mother goat breaks into the yam store her kid watches her. — Igbo

Admiration is the daughter of ignorance.

— American

Adversity

If your part of the battlefield is covered with thorns, you do not leave your position and go to stand where the ground is good. — Twi

Daag da sweat, but long hair cover him.

— Jamaican

No sooner has one pushed one gourd under water than another pops up.

— Chinese

Misfortune conquers timid souls while great minds subdue misfortune.

— Chinese

That which is quickly acquired is easily lost.

— Chinese

The lotus springs from the mud.

— Chinese

If you never go up a hill, you will never know what a plain is like.

— Chinese

The greater your troubles, the greater is your opportunity to show yourself a worthy person.

— Chinese

Our enemies teach us life's most valuable lessons.

— Chinese

Remove the stone and you won't stumble.
Quitando la piedra, se quita el tropezon. — Belize

God promises a safe landing, but not a calm passage.

— English

Adversity makes strange bedfellows.

— English

Prosperity gets followers, but adversity distinguishes them.

— English

There is no little enemy.   — American

Adversity flatters no man.   — American

Advice

She who ignores advice does not resist when being
prepared for burial.   — Kikuyu

If you are not told about it, you go among
people soiled.   — Ovambo

One who refused advice was later seen bleeding.
                                           — Shona

Stream said that it is because it has nobody to
direct it that . . . it goes in a zigzag way.
                                           — Igbo

It's a fine sermon about fasting when the preacher just had lunch.

Buena predica de ayuno es la del que acaba del almorzar. — Ecuadoran

Though you possess prudence, old man, do not despise advice. — Panamanian

Better a finger off than one wagging.

— English

We hate those who will not take our advice and despise those who do. — American

Advice is least heeded when most needed.

— American

Advice, like water, takes the form of the vessel it is poured into. — American

Less advice and more hands.   — American

Afterlife

In death I am born.   — Hopi

Sing your death song and die like a hero
going home.   — Shawnee

The dead add their strength and counsel
to the living.   — Hopi

Life is not separate from death. It only looks
that way.   — Blackfoot

Many are the roads by which God brings his own
to heaven.   — Venezuelan

There is no leaping from Delilah's lap into
Abraham's bosom.   — American

Age

Grow old, body, the heart still remains.

— Ndebele

The one who used to jump across the stream may find herself wading through. — Kikuyu

Plantain ripe, can't green again. — Jamaican

You can run away from your elder, but she'll outthink you. — Sukuma

The child looks everywhere and often sees naught; the old man, sitting on the ground, sees everything. — Wolof

Eyes that see do not grow old.

— Nicaraguan

The child weeps for its good and the old man for his ill.   — Peruvian

He who runs in his youth, trots in his old age.
El que de joven corre, de viejo trota.   — Spanish

Youth is intoxication without wine; old age, wine without intoxication.   — Peruvian

The devil's wiser more on account of his age than on account of being the devil.
Más sabe el diablo por viejo que por diablo.
                                                                    — Ecuadoran

Youth does not mind where it sets its foot.
Is cuma leis an óige cá leagann sí a cos.   — Irish

Youth sheds many a skin.
Is iomaí craiceanna chuireas an óige di.   — Irish

Death is in front of the old person and at the back of the young person.
Bíonn an bás ar aghaidh an tseanduine agus ar chúl an duine óig.   — Irish

Praise the young and they will flourish.
Mol an óige agus tiocfaidh sí.   — Irish

Age is honorable and youth is noble.
Tá onóir ag an aois agus uaisle ag an óige.
                                  — Irish

The beginning and end of one's life is to draw closer to the fire.
Tús agus deireadh an duine duine tarringt ar an tine.   — Irish

Youth will have its fling.
Ni thagann ciall roimh aois.   — Irish

64

If youth but knew and age but could do.
Si gioventú sapesse e se vecchiaia potesse.

— Italian

A horse which is tamed at forty is only good for resurrection day. — Arabic

Don't send an old man to buy a donkey, nor a young man to woo a wife. — Arabic

Old age is a thousand headaches. — Arabic

He's auld an' cauld an' ill to lie beside.

— Scottish

Auld wives and bairns [*children*] mak fools o' physicians. — Scottish

A good goose indeed, but she was an ill gaislin.
                                        — Scottish

There's nae iron sae hard but rust will fret it;
there's nae claith sae fine but moths will eat it.
                                        — Scottish

A young tree bends, an old tree breaks.
Ah yunguer boim baigr zich, an alter boim vert
tzubrochen.   — Hebrew

Like lavender, grow sweeter as you grow older.
                                        — English

Eternity has no grey hairs.   — English

A man may die old at thirty and young at eighty.
                                        — English

An old wrinkle never wears out.   — English

They who would be young when they are old
must be old when they are young.   — English

Age and wedlock bring a man to his nightcap.
                                          — English

Youth will be served.   — English

Age lasts; youth devours.   — American

Age and marriage tame man and beast.
                                          — American

Every age wants its playthings.   — American

Ambition

When the hare leaps, there are no lame greyhounds.
Cuando salta la liebre no hay galgos cojos.

— Venezuelan

Lawyer for the rich, scourge of the poor.
Abogado de ricos, mal de pobres.   — Peruvian

In the boss's eyes you'll always see ambition.
En los ojos del patron veras siempre la ambicion.

— Puerto Rican

Ambition spills the sack.
La ambicion rompe el saco.   — Chilean

Boat-swalling fish do not live in brooks.
Donshu-no-uo wa sairyu ni sumazu.   — Japanese

A whip even to a galloping horse.
Hashiru uma ni mo muchi. — Japanese

If you become a dog, turn into a dog of a
wealthy family.
Inu ni naru nara odokora no inu ni nare.
— Japanese

In a wealthy man's house there is no lean dog.
Tomu ie ni yase inu nashi. — Japanese

He who is anxious to secure the best tends to get
stuck with the worst of the rest.
*El que ansioso escoge lo mejor suele quedarse con
lo peor.* — Mexican

Ambition never has its fill.
La ambición nunca se llena. — Mexican

For whoever wants the blue sky, the price is high.
El que quiere azul celeste, que le cueste.

— Mexican

Ambition is putting a ladder against the sky.

— American

A man without ambition is like a woman
without looks.

— American

Anger

A small pot boils quickly.

— Swahili

In anger there is no intelligence.

— Sukuma

By getting angry, one shows that she is wrong.

— Malagasy

When you lift your hand to strike, you are three-tenths lower than your opponent.   — Chinese

The sea of bitterness has no bounds—repent and the shore is near.   — Chinese

Do not create in anger what you lack in reason.
      — Chinese

The little pot is soonest hot.   — Chinese

All kinds of hellish devils rule an angry person.
Kol ha'ko'es kol meenai gaiheenom sholteem bo.
      — Hebrew

Don't be quick to get angry; rage is found in the bosom of fools.
Al tivahel b'ruchacha lichos, kee ka'as b'chaik k'seeleem yanuach.   — Hebrew

A person slow to anger has great understanding;
one with a quick temper exalts foolishness.
Erech apayeem rav-t'vuna, uk'tzar ru'ach
mereem ivelet. — Hebrew

Words of the mouth are like a stone in a sling.
— Mexican

Malice leaves reality behind.
La malicia va más allá de la realidad.
— Mexican

Blood boils without flame.
La sangre sin fuego hierve. — Mexican

Wounds from the knife are healed, but not those
from the tongue. — Mexican

Even a small mouse has anger.
— Tribe Unknown

In anger a man becomes dangerous to himself and
to others.   — Omaha

Do not allow anger to poison you.   — Hopi

An angry word is like striking with a knife.
                                              — Hopi

If someone hates you, don't let her find
you hateful.   — Tshi

Anger in a house is like a worm in a plant.
                                              — Hebrew

A soft answer turns away anger.
Muchadh feirge sofhreagra.   — Irish

No man is angry that feels not himself hurt.
                                              — English

The anger is not warrantable that has seen
two suns.   — English

Two things a man should never get angry at: what
he can help and what he cannot.   — English

A good remedy for anger is delay.   — American

Beware the anger of a patient man.   — American

Animals

The squirrel can beat the rabbit climbing a tree,
but then the rabbit makes the best stew and that
sort of equalizes the thing.   — African American

What would you expect from an ass but a kick?
Cad é bheadh súil agat a fháil ó bhó ach preab?
                                          — Irish

Better is an ass that carries you than a horse that
throws you.
Is fearr asal a iomchras thú ná capall a chaitheas thú.
— Irish

It is easy to drive with your own whip and
another's horse.
Do fhuip féin is capall na comharsan. — Irish

He who has cattle on the hill will not sleep easy.
An té a bhfuil bólacht ar cnoc aige ní bhíonn
suaimhneas ar sop aige. — Irish

"Every man to his fancy, and me to my own
fancy," said the old woman when she kissed
her cow. — Irish

It is a bad hen can't scrape for herself.
Is olc an chearch nach scriobann di fein. — Irish

The grace of God is found between the saddle and the ground.
Bionn grasta De idir an diallait agus an talamh.

— Irish

It's natural for ducks to go barefoot.
Se duchas na lachan snamh.

— Irish

If one sheep puts his head through the gap the rest will follow.
An rud a níos gabhar déanfaidh gabhar eile é.

— Irish

When your hand is in the dog's mouth, withdraw it gently.
An uair a bhíonn do lámh i mbéal an mhadra, tarraing go réidh í.

— Irish

Don't go putting wool on a sheep's back.
*Is dona an rud an iomarca saille a chur ar dhroim
muice beathaithe.* — Irish

When you see a goat you should always hit him,
because he is either going into mischief or coming
out of it. — Irish

If you put a silk suit on a goat it is still a goat.
Cuir síoda ar ghabhar is ghabhar i gcónaí é.
— Irish

Keep the bone and the dog will follow.
Coinnigh an cnámh agus leanfaidh an madadh thú.
— Irish

When the cat is out, the mouse can dance.
*Nuair bhíos an cat amuigh, bíonn cead rince ag na
luchóga.* — Irish

Every cock can crow on his own dunghill.
Is teann gach coileach ar a charn aoiligh féin.

— Irish

A bird flies high above and its funeral is
performed on the ground.   — Mamprussi

The goat is not big in a cow town.   — Vai

Wherever there are bones, there are dogs.

— Jamaican

Alligator lay egg but him no fowl.

— Jamaican

Do not try to fight a lion if you are not one
yourself.   — Swahili

It is mysterious if a baboon falls from a tree.

— Shona

You can have no more of a cat than her skin.

— English

You should lie down with the lamb and rise with the lark.

— English

Do not dwell in a city where a horse does not neigh nor a dog bark.

— English

It is the trapped animal that makes the most noise.

— American

Anxiety

A person worries about the past, is upset about the present, and fears the future.

Adam do'eg le'avar, niv'hal lhoveh, v'yareh le'ateed.

— Hebrew

The cure for anxiety about the future is not
nostalgia for the past.   — Hebrew

To carry care to bed is to sleep with a pack on
your back.   — American

Appearance

A silk dress doesn't mean clean undergarments.
                                             — Haitian

Patching makes a garment last long.
                                             — Yoruban

The cook does not have to be a beautiful woman.
                                             — Shona

A man possesses beauty in his quality and a
woman possesses quality in her beauty.

                                             — Cuban

The beauty of the man is in his intelligence and the intelligence of the woman is in her beauty.

— Bolivian

No matter if the child's born with a flat nose, as long as it breathes. — Ecuadoran

A mirror doesn't know how to lie.
Un espejo no sabe ser embustero. — Haitian

Dress the monkey in silk and it is still a monkey.

— Argentinean

Beauty is only skin deep, ugliness goes to the bone.
Ní théann áilleacht thar an gcraiceann. — Irish

Beauty never boiled the pot and ugliness never thickened it.
Cha chuireann maise an pota ar gail. — Irish

An inch is a great deal on a nose.
Is mór orlach de shrón duine. — Irish

Many an honest heart beats under a ragged coat.
Is minic a bhí croí fíor fá chasóg stróicthe.
— Irish

You cannot tell from a man's clothes how much he is making, but you must look at his wife's.
— Irish

The shoemaker's wife and the blacksmith's horse often go unshod.
Is minic drochbhróga ar bhean gréasaí. — Irish

Many a white collar covers a dirty neck. — Irish

Any fool carries an umbrella on a wet day, but the wise man carries it every day.
Bearfaidh an fear críonna a chóta leis lá tirim.
— Irish

The cowl does not make the monk.
L'abito non fa il monaco. — Italian

One swallow does not make a spring.
Una rondine non fa primavera. — Italian

Dress up a stick and it does not appear to be a stick.
Vesti un legno, pare un regno. — Italian

Beauty and folly are old companions.
Bellezza e follia vanno spesso in compagnia.
— Italian

A beautiful ornament looks best on a beautiful woman.
— Hebrew

In a community, your reputation matters. In a strange place, your clothing counts.
— Hebrew

Three things please a man: a lovely home, a lovely wife, and lovely possessions.
Shlosha marcheeveem da'ato shel adam: deera na'ah, eesha na'ah, v'kaileem na'eem.
— Hebrew

Ten measures of beauty descended on the world; nine went to Jerusalem, and one to the rest of the world.
Asara kobeen yofee yardu la'olam, tisha natla yerushalayeem v'echad kol ha'olam kulo.
— Hebrew

There is no greater beauty than that of logic.
Ain hidur c'hidur higayon. — Hebrew

Don't be afraid of the chili pepper, even though it's so red.
No le tengan miedo al chile aunque lo vean colorado.
— Mexican

Although a monkey be dressed in silk, she is still a monkey. — Mexican

There's no better mirror than an old friend.
No hay mejor espejo que el amigo viejo.
— Mexican

Afar, it enraptures the heart, when near, it rends the gallbladder. — Arabic

Outer beauty is no good, give me inner beauty.

— Arabic

God sends clothes to those with no proper figure, and bread to those with no teeth. — Arabic

An ugly woman's husband better be blind.

— Arabic

If you're beautiful, whatever you do is fine.

— Arabic

A God-given beauty needs no beautician.

— Arabic

An excellent appearance, an empty pocket.

— Arabic

If you dress in gold or silk, you are still the same
green grocer.   — Arabic

A' Stuarts are no sib to the King.   — Scottish

Better be deid than oot o' fashion.   — Scottish

Beauty's muck when honour's tint.   — Scottish

An ilka-day braw maks a Sabbath-day daw.
                                               — Scottish

A broken leg is not healed by a silk stocking.
                                               — English

Ever since we wear clothes, we know not each
other.   — English

Arrogance

It's as if she's fallen off an elephant's trunk.

— Arabic

Self-praise is like chewing cotton wool. — Arabic

Don't pride over your wealth or beauty, one will
be gone in a night and the other with a fever.

— Arabic

He who spits towards the sky is spitting on
his face.   — Igbo

Arrogance is a kingdom without a crown.

— American

The weed of arrogance grows on a dunghill.

— American

Authenticity

Crows weep for the dead lamb then devour him.

Il corvo piange la pecora e poi la mangia.

— Italian

A flatterer's throat is an open sepulchre.

Gola degli adulatori, sepolcro aperto. — Italian

It is not by saying, "honey, honey," that sweetness comes into the mouth.

Non é col dire "miel, miel," che la dolcezza viene in bocca. — Italian

Must is a king's word. — English

Authority/Leadership

Cat no deh, ratta tek over. — Guyanan

What is decided by legitimate authority is not
resented by the subjects.   — Gandan

De tune you playing no de one I dancing.
                                          — Jamaican

If the people of the town and village are all happy,
look for the chief.   — Krahn

Although the horse is stupid, it does not follow
that the rider is stupid.   — Tshi

Where there is a herd without a bull, a castrated
ox will rule.   — Boran

Eagles fly alone.   — English

Authority without wisdom is like a heavy axe
without an edge.   — American

To command one must learn to obey.

— American

Barter

It is a poor village that has neither smoke nor fire.
Is baile bocht baile gan toit gan tine.   — Irish

Money is like muck—no good till spread.

— Irish

Money makes the horse gallop whether he has
shoes or not.   — Irish

Forgetting a debt does not pay it.
Ní dhíolann dearmhad fiacha.   — Irish

A penny in a poor man's pocket is better than two
pennies in a rich man's pocket.   — Irish

Your pocket is your friend.
Is é do phóca do charaid. — Irish

Don't bring all your eggs to one market.
Na cuir do chuid uibheacha uilig in aon bhosca amhain. — Irish

Go to a man who is in difficulty and you'll get a bargain.
Druid le fear na broid agus gheobhair conradh.
— Irish

Long fingers count out money. — English

What cannot gold do? — English

Beauty

Cherry blossoms in the recesses of a mountain.
Miyama no sakura. — Japanese

A red lacquer dish needs no decoration.
Tanshitsu kazarazu. — Japanese

An eight-sided beauty is coldhearted.
Happo bijin wa hakujo. — Japanese

Some people clean a tap an' dutty underneath.
— Jamaican

Beautiful 'ooman [*woman*], beautiful trouble.
— Jamaican

Beauty widout grace like rose widout smell.
— Jamaican

That which in the beautiful woman is grace, in
the ugly woman turns to disgrace.
Lo que en la bonita es gracia en la fea es desgracia.
— El Salvadoran

Beauty and folly are constant companions.
La belleza y la tonteria van siempre en compania.
— Costa Rican

Prettiness dies first. — English

Beauty provoketh thieves sooner than gold.
— English

Beauty without virtue is a rose without fragrance.
— American

Bravery

Faint heart never won fair lady.
Amante no sará, chi coraggio non ha.　　　— Italian

Even Homer sometimes nods.
Qualche volta anche Omero sonnecchia.
　　　　　　　　　　　　　　　　— Italian

It's not so terrible when you lose money. When
courage is lost, all is lost.
*Farloirene guelt nit gueferlech. Farloirene mut, als iz
farloiren.*　　　　　　　　　　　— Yiddish

Who can find a woman of valor? Her price is far
above rubies.　　　　　　　　　　— Hebrew

Those who train themselves in wisdom cultivate
true courage.　　　　　　　　　　— Hebrew

He's as bold as a Lammermuir lion.

— Scottish

Every man for his ain hand, as Henry Wynd
fought.　　　　　　　　　　　　　 — Scottish

Even a haggis will run downhill.　　　 — Scottish

None but the brave deserve the fair.　 — English

It is easy to be brave from a safe distance.

— American

True bravery is without witness.　　 — American

Business

If lending were a good idea, then the husband
would lend out his wife.
*Eelu haya tov b'hash'eel kee az haya masheel haba'al
et ishto.*   — Hebrew

Lend money and acquire an enemy.
                                              — Yiddish

A borrower may not lend the thing he borrowed.
                                              — Hebrew

When prices drop, buy.   — Hebrew

Forget brotherhood, each goat will cost you
seven dinars.   — Arabic

Eat your bread with water and don't ask for
another's dough.   — Arabic

The goat does not get fat just by whispering.

— Arabic

To put Taghi's hat on Naghi's head.   — Arabic

Account by the dinar, give charity by the assload.

— Arabic

Money finds money, water finds the puddle.

— Arabic

As ane flits anither fits, and that keeps mailins
dear.   — Scottish

If you would be a merchant fine, beware o' auld
horses, herring, and wine.   — Scottish

He cuts awfu' near the wood.   — Scottish

Dreigh bargains bode ill. — Scottish

Did ye ever fit counts wi' him? — Scottish

Buying and selling is but winning and losing.
— English

They who have much business must have much
pardon. — English

The fingers have got pretty close to the thumb.
— English

Business first, pleasure after. — English

The citizen is at his business before the sun rises.
— English

Turn the cake in the pan.   — English

Cheese and money should always sleep together
one night.   — English

Nothing is lost in a good market.   — English

Good weight and measure are heaven's treasure.
                                               — American

Business goes where it is invited and stays where it
is well treated.   — American

Business neglected is business lost.
                                               — American

Caution

Being careful is not being a coward.   — Haitian

Cockroach neber so drunk him walk a
fowl yard.   — Jamaican

Man dat carry straw no fe fool wid fire.
                — Jamaican

No one tests the depth of the river with both feet.
                — Krahn

Flies can't fall in[to] a tight-closed pot.
                — African American

I'm not going to lend you a stick to break my
head with.   — African American

He who shows a passion tells his enemy where he may hit him. — Colombian

A lame man always speaks when it's time to run.
Siempre habla un cojo cuando hay que correr.
— Colombian

Beware of one with a honeyed tongue and a sword in the belly. — Chinese

Don't be a tiger's head with a snake's tail.
— Chinese

It takes more than one cold day for a river to freeze three feet deep. — Chinese

Be slow to promise but quick to perform.
— Chinese

Never rub your eye but with your elbow.
Gli occhi s'hanno a toccare con le gomita.

— Italian

The lone sheep is in danger of the wolf.
La pecora che se ne va sola, il lupo la mangia.

— Italian

Not even Hercules could contend against two.
Contro due non la potrebbe Orlando.   — Italian

A basic rule of caution: Don't be overly cautious.
*Maichukai hazeheerut hu livlee lihizaher
yoter midei.*

— Hebrew

Three need to be guarded: A patient, a groom,
and a bride.   — Hebrew

Don't be [*too*] sweet lest people lick you.
Al t'hee matok v'timatzetz. — Hebrew

Before you choose a counselor, watch him with
his neighbor's children. — Sioux

Beware of the man who does not talk and the dog
that does not bark. — Cheyenne

You must always be careful with something that is
greater than you are. — Shoshone

A danger foreseen is half-avoided.

— Cheyenne

Never go to sleep when your meat is on the fire.
— Pueblo

Go softly, come softly, so that the cat does not
gore you.   — Arabic

When a life is at stake, don't follow the majority.
Ain holcheen b'fiku'ach nefesh acharai harov.
                                         — Hebrew

Rocking chairs make long-tailed cats uneasy.
                                         — Mexican

Better a steady drip than a sudden deluge.
                                         — Mexican

The lap of its owner is security enough for a cat.
                                         — Mexican

Don't do good that could look bad.
No hagas cosas buenas que parezcan malas.
— Mexican

No road is safer than the one just robbed.
*No hay camino más seguro que el que acaban
de robar.* — Mexican

A man forewarned is equal to two. — Mexican

Wait 'til your ass crosses the bridge. — Arabic

That is the lion's tail, do not play with it.
— Arabic

Three things to fear: a crumbling wall, an angry
dog, and a shrew. — Arabic

Out of desperation he calls the cat "Madam"!

— Arabic

Barefooted folk shouldna tread on thorns.

— Scottish

Save yourself frae the deil and the laird's bairns.

— Scottish

Let aye the bell'd wether break the snaw.

— Scottish

Bees that hae honey in their mouths hae stings in their tails.

— Scottish

The butterfly that brushes against thorns will tear its wings.

— Yoruban

The rat knows full well that, if the cat is old and feeble, its claws are not. — Haitian

Tread on the ball [*of the foot*], live to spend all.
— English

Beware beginnings. — English

He that plays with cats must expect to be scratched. — English

People with wax heads shouldn't walk in the sun.
— English

Caution is the downfall to ambition.
— American

Young courage and old caution are a strong pair.
— American

Change

Ebery day debil help tief, one day God help
watchman. — Jamaican

Night is followed by day, famine by abundance.
— Ovambo

When a person is not as she used to be, she does
not behave as she used to behave. — Igbo

A change is as good as a rest. — English

All things change and we with them.
— English

Change of fortune hurts a wise man no more than
a change of the moon. — American

Character

Empty barrel mek de mos' noise.   — Jamaican

When rain beats on a leopard it wets it, but rain does not wash out its spots.   — Ashanti

A lame of heart is not a lame of leg; he cannot be recognized.   — Kikuyu

The house of the loud talker leaks.   — Zulu

As soon as the monkey has climbed a tree, it will start abusing from its elevated position.

     — Namibian

Wagon makes the loudest noise when it's goin' out empty.   — African American

Competent by inheritance, incompetent by
character.   — Hausan

Blood is inherited and virtue is acquired.
                                        — Venezuelan

The strong forgive, the weak remember.
                                        — Ecuadoran

There is no better friend than a burden.
                                        — Colombian

Tell me what company you keep and I will tell
you who you are.   — Cuban

Join with good men and you will be one of them.
                                        — Venezuelan

Tell me with whom you go and I'll tell you what
you are.
Dimmi con chi vai, e ti diró che fai [chi sei].
— Italian

He who makes an idol of his interest makes a
martyr of his integrity.
*Chi si fa un idolo del suo interesse, si fa un martire
della sua integritá.* — Italian

If your heart is bitter, sugar in the mouth won't
help.
*Oib siz biter in hartz'n, vet tzuker in moil nit
helf'n.* — Yiddish

A slave shows his true character, not while he is
enslaved but when he becomes a master.
*Ha'eved m'galeh et teevo ha'ameetee, teva ha'eved, lo
bihiyoto eved, kee eem b'he'asoto l'adon.*

— Hebrew

A people's legends reveal its character more clearly
than its acts and events.
*Agodatav shel am m'galot lanu et yofyo yuoter
mishehu misfaleh b'ma'asai ha'am u'v'mikrav.*
— Hebrew

Three things show a man's character: his drinking,
his pocket, and his anger.
*Bishlosha d'vareem ha'adam nikar: koso, keeso,
ka'aso.* — Hebrew

It's hard to know the quality of a person, or a
watermelon.
*Gam avatee ach v' gam adam kesheh la' amod miyad
al reevam.* — Japanese

Worth makes the man and want of it the fellow.
— Mexican

By the claw you may know the lion.

— Mexican

Self-praise amounts to self-condemnation.
Alabanza en boca propia es vituperio. — Mexican

An empty bag will not stay up.
Costal vacío no se para. — Mexican

Great deeds are reserved for great men.

— Mexican

No one else can represent your conscience.

— Anishinabe

If a man is as wise as a serpent he can afford to be
as harmless as a dove. — Cheyenne

There are many good moccasin tracks along the
trail of a straight arrow.   — Fox

How can the eater of dates forbid the eating
of dates?   — Arabic

Though pepper is a tiny thing, its taste is mighty
powerful.   — Arabic

He's hardly a sour grape, yet behaves like a raisin.
                                              — Arabic

He'll gang mad on a horse wha's proud on
a pownie.   — Scottish

They that see but your head dinna see your
height.   — Scottish

It's stinking praise comes oot o' ane's own mouth.
— Scottish

When your character is made, you may lie a-bed.
— English

Character is what you are in the dark when no one else is around.
— American

If it looks like a duck, walks like a duck, and quacks like a duck, it's probably a duck.
— American

Charity

A thread from everyone will make a shirt for the needy.
— Russian

Charity bread has hard crusts.
— English

Send your charity abroad wrapped in blankets.

— English

God loves him who cares for the poor more than
him who respects the wealthy.

— Ancient Egyptian

Almsgiving never impoverished, stealing never
enriched, and prosperity never made wise.

— English

What is bought is cheaper than a gift.

— English

Charity is a virtue of the heart and not of
the hand.   — American

Charity is not a bone you throw to your dog but a
bone you share with your dog.   — American

117

Children

Children are poor men's riches.
I figli sono la ricchezza dei poveri. — Italian

Marry your son when you will, your daughter
when you can.
Accasa il figlio quando vuoi, e la figlia quando puoi.
— Italian

The ones that matter most are the children. They
are the true human beings. — Lakota

It takes a whole village to raise a child.
— Omaha

Talk to your children while they are eating; what
you say will stay even after you are gone.
— Nez Perce

A man or woman with many children has
many homes.   — Lakota

Take your children with you where you go and be
not ashamed.   — Hopi

Remember that your children are not your own,
but are lent to you by the Creator.   — Mohawk

As a crab walks, so walk its children.   — Kpelle

Small children, a headache; big children,
heartache.
Hak'taneen, c'ev rosh; hag'doleem, c'ev lev.
                                     — Hebrew

If you do not honor your parents, your children will not honor you.

Eem lo t'chabed horecha, lo y'chabducha banecha.
— Hebrew

Bairns speak i' the field what they hear i' the ha'.
— Scottish

Christiecreek will come to ye.　　　— Scottish

A child may have too much of his mother's blessing.
— English

If you rock the cradle empty, then you shall have babies plenty.
— English

With one child you may walk; with two you may ride; when you have three, at home you must bide. — English

A man among children will long be a child; a child among men will soon be a man. — English

Children and fools must not play with edged tools. — English

Children are certain cares, but uncertain comforts. — English

A babe is a mother's anchor; she cannot swing from her moorings. — American

A mother's heart is a child's schoolroom. — American

Choices

If one comes to a fork of the road in a strange country, she stops to think. — Jabo

If you have decided to eat a dog, eat a fat one. — Ugandan

If you sleep under a tree, you can't prevent the leaf from falling on you. — Haitian

One cannot drink and whistle at once.
Non si può bere e fischiare. — Italian

To err is human, to persist in it, beastly.
Errare é umano, ma perdurare nell'errore diabolico. — Italian

He who begins many things, finishes but few.
Chi troppo comincia, poco finisce. — Italian

When in doubt of what is right, consult your
pillow overnight.
Cuando en duda, consúltado con tu almohada.
— Mexican

As to tastes, nothing is written.
Sobre gustos no hay nada escrito.   — Mexican

There is no choosing between two things of
no value.   — Mexican

Everyone has their own way of killing fleas.
Cada quien tiene su forma de matar a pulgas.
— Mexican

Never interfere in a person's decisions about what
he will do with his possessions.   — Hopi

Those who have one foot in the canoe and one
foot in the boat are going to fall into the river.

— Tuscaroran

Grapes and grapes! — Arabic

What can an old harlot do but repent of her
misdeeds? — Arabic

When you cannot bite a hand, kiss it.

— Arabic

Two watermelons cannot be carried in one hand.

— Arabic

It's hard to make a choice between two blind dogs.
Is deacair rogha a bhaint as dhar ghabhar chaocha.

— Irish

Forced put is no choice. — English

There is small choice in rotten apples.

— English

The obvious choice is usually a quick regret.

— American

Common Sense

When you see clouds gathering, prepare to catch rainwater. — Golan

The insane are told they're right.
A los locos se les da la razón. — Mexican

If you're going to rest under the sun, it's better to keep walking.
Para descansar bajo el sol, es mejor seguir andando.

— Mexican

There's no reason to walk on the branches when the trunk is so thick.

No hay que andarse por las ramas estando tan grueso el tronco.   — Mexican

If you would be a good judge, pay attention to what everyone says.   — Mexican

The brains of a fox will be of little service if you play with the paw of a lion.   — English

Commonality

Languages differ but coughs are the same.

— Nigerian

It is a thief that can trace the footsteps of another thief on a rock.   — Yoruban

Wherever you go, the sky is the same color.
— Arabic

When you mention "dog," you should get a stick.
— Arabic

Likeness is the mother of love.   — English

In every country dogs bite.   — English

Community

As you live yourself, you judge your neighbor.
*Mar chaitheas duine a bheatha, tabhair breith ar
a chomharsain.*   — Irish

Don't break your shins on your neighbors' pots.
— Italian

Never want while your neighbor has it.

— Italian

Everyone is nice till the cow gets into the garden.
Bíonn gach duine lách go dtéann bó ina gharraí.

— Irish

Don't take a slate off your own house to put on
your neighbor's.
*Ná bain tuí de do thoigh féin le sclátaí a chur ar
thoigh fir eile.* — Irish

Don't outstay your welcome like a neighbor's goat.
Cuairt ghearr is imeacht buíoch. — Irish

If you want to know me, come and live with me.
Níl eolas gan aontíos. — Irish

Join the community: the wolf snatches only the stray sheep that wanders off from the flock.
Hitchaber el hatzibur she'harai haz'ev yachtof min ha'eder hakivsa hato'a l'vad. — Hebrew

The community is Israel's rampart. — Hebrew

Good company will save you from bad deeds.
Hachavura hatova matzelet min hara'ot.
— Hebrew

From the fallen tree everyone makes firewood.
Del árbol caído todos hacen leña. — Mexican

Conversation is food for the soul.
La conversación es el pasto del alma. — Mexican

Better one timely squawk than constant talk.
*Vale más un grito a tiempo que hablar a cada
momento.* — Mexican

A people without a history is like the wind over
buffalo grass. — Sioux

Work hard, keep the ceremonies, live peaceably,
and unite your hearts. — Hopi

First you are to think always of God. Second you
are to use all your powers to care for your people
and especially the poor. — Sioux

A people without faith in themselves cannot
survive. — Hopi

A crowd is not company. — English

Comparison

Threaten him with death so that he may be
content with fever.   — Arabic

Each Hajji [*pilgrim*] goes to Mecca his own way.
                                       — Arabic

A flow will have an ebb.   — English

Comparisons make enemies of our friends.
                                       — American

Completion

"I nearly killed the bird." No one can eat "nearly"
in a stew.   — Yoruban

I have sifted my flour and hung up the sieve.
                                       — Arabic

He makes a hundred knives, none of which has
a handle.   — Arabic

It is the end of the Shahnameh [*an epic Persian
poem*] that is pleasant.   — Arabic

A cast is not a catch.   — English

Compromise

One who would pick the roses must bear with
the thorns.   — Chinese

Compromise is always a temporary achievement.
                                                   — Chinese

You must lose a fly to catch a trout.   — English

Better bend the back than bruise the forehead.

— English

Compromise makes a good umbrella but a
poor roof.   — American

Conduct

Inquire about everything that you may understand
it. Be good tempered and magnanimous, that
your disposition may be attractive.

— Ancient Egyptian

One who is serious all day will never have a good
time, while one who is frivolous all day will never
establish a household.   — Ancient Egyptian

When a child knows how to wash his hands well,
he eats with the elders.   — Tshi

When you know that people are watching you, there are things that you don't do. — Haitian

He preaches well that lives well. — English

If a man is right, he cannot be too radical; if wrong, he cannot be too conservative.

— American

Confidence

To be praised is to be ruined. — Kikuyu

The bocor [*medicine man*] gives you a protective charm, but he doesn't tell you to sleep in the middle of the highway. — Haitian

Confidence of success is almost success.

— American

Conflict

The lance never blunted the pen, nor the pen the lance.　　　　　　　— Nicaraguan

Whether the pitcher strike the stone or the stone the pitcher, the pitcher suffers.　　— Panamanian

Choose the stone by the size of the frog.
Según el sapo es la pedrada.　　　　　— Honduran

One sword keeps another in its scabbard.
　　　　　　　　　　　　　　— Venezuelan

A weapon is an enemy even to its owner.
　　　　　　　　　　　　　　— Guatemalan

There's no agreement under pressure.
Bajo presión no hay acuerdo.　　　　— Cuban

Force may lead to agreement, but truth will lead to conviction.   — Chinese

Tenacity and adversity are old foes.   — Chinese

Ones who are unable to live under the same sky.
                                                            — Chinese

To a man prepared for war, peace is assured.
D'fhear cogaidh comhaltar síocháin.   — Irish

The man of courage never lost it.
Níor chaill fear an mhisnigh riamh é.   — Irish

A good retreat is better than a poor fight.
Is fearr rith maith ná drochsheasamh.   — Irish

Let him who will not take advice have conflict.
An té ná gabhann comhairle gabhadh sé comhrac.
                                                             — Irish

Reverence ceases once blood is spilt.
Ní théann urraim thar dhoirteadh fola. — Irish

Trust not a spiteful man.
Ná tabhair taobh le fear fala. — Irish

Do not show your teeth until you can bite.
Ná nocht d'fhiacla go bhféadfair an greim do bhreith. — Irish

Rarely is a fight continued when the chief has fallen.
Ní gnách cosaint ar díth tiarna. — Irish

No matter who comes off well, the peacemaker is sure to come off ill.
Cibé a théann as nó nach dtéann, ní théann fear na hidirghabhála. — Irish

Nothing that is violent is permanent.
Violenza non dura a lungo. — Italian

He who strikes first strikes twice.
El que da primero da dos veces. — Mexican

Let him attack who will; the strong wait.
— Mexican

There's no worse struggle than one that never begins.
No hay peor lucha que la que no se hace.
— Mexican

To win a dispute is to gain a chicken and lose a cow.
Ganar un pleito es adquirir un pollo y perder una vaca. — Mexican

He who punishes one chastises a hundred.

— Mexican

There can never be peace between nations until
it is first known that true peace is within the souls
of men. — Oglala Sioux

Make my enemy brave and strong, so that if
defeated, I will not be ashamed.

— Plains Indian

There was never a conflict without a woman.

— English

It takes two blows to make a battle.

— English

Use soft words and hard arguments.

— English

To fight once shows bravery, but to fight all the time is stupid. — Oromo

A blow is repaid by the like of it, and all that is achieved is a hitting. — Ancient Egyptian

If he has thrown the only spear he had at you, it means that he doesn't fear you.

— Ugandan

The mouth which ate pepper is the one which pepper affected. — Idoman

He who provokes a war must be sure that he knows how to fight. — Tsongan

A man that will fight will find a cudgel in every hedge. — English

Consequences

The throat must pay for what the tongue may say.
— Mexican

He who follows his own advice must take the
consequences.   — Mexican

The frog squashed the hardest croaks the loudest.
La rana mas aplastada es la que más recio grita.
— Mexican

The rat that knows but one hole is soon caught by
the cat.   — Mexican

Everything wears away from use.
Todo por servir se acaba.   — Mexican

He is not to blame who does his duty.
— Mexican

Do not wrong or hate your neighbor, for it is not he that you wrong but yourself. — Piman

The soul would have no rainbow if the eyes had no tears. — Minquass

If you dig a pit for me, you dig one for yourself. — Creole

The jar broke and the wine spilled. — Arabic

When you play, you may break your head. — Arabic

Do good and throw it in the Tigris and God will repay you in the desert. — Arabic

He who spits up in the air will get it back on his beard. — Arabic

Don't neglect the consequence of your act.

— Arabic

He that sows the wind shall reap the whirlwind.

— Arabic

Cooperation

If everyone helps to hold up the sky, then one person does not become tired.   — Tshi

The attempt exceeds the ability of one, not of a multitude.   — Efik

The hand of the child cannot reach the shelf, nor the hand of the adult get through the neck of the gourd.   — Yoruban

A beautiful flower is incomplete without its leaves.

— Chinese

One sings, all follow.   — Chinese

A single tree cannot make a forest.   — Chinese

Hard with hard makes not the stone wall.
Duro con duro non fa buon muro.   — Italian

He who is unyielding in a dispute is a sinner.
                                          — Hebrew

Many hands can shatter stout walls.
Rabot hayadayeem m'shabrot chomotayeem.
                                          — Hebrew

Untying one of two ropes tied together means you
untie both.
Ishterai chad chevel, isherai train chavaleem.
                                          — Hebrew

They were two, but united; we were a hundred,
but divided.   — Arabic

From you the money, from me the dance.
                                                — Arabic

Gnats, in great number, can beat an elephant.
                                                — Arabic

It was not on one foot that St. Patrick came to
Ireland.
Ni ar anon chois a thainig Padraig go Érirnn.
                                                — Irish

Two shorten the road.
Giorraionn beirt bothar.   — Irish

Courage

The brave one lives as long as the coward lets him.
El valiente vive hasta que el cobarde quiere.

— Mexican

Better to die on your feet than to live on
your knees.
Más vale morir parado que vivir de rodillas.

— Mexican

A brave dies but once—a coward many times.

— Iowa

Death is nothing and pain is nothing, but
cowardice is crime and disgrace, the greatest
punishment.   — Dakota

Be brave where bravery is honorable.

— Assiniboine

One has to face fear or forever run from it.

— Crow

Moscow does not believe in tears.   — Russian

When the fight's over, don't wave your fists.

— Russian

Vows made in storms are forgotten in calms.

— Russian

Without danger we cannot get beyond danger.

— English

A man of courage never wants weapons.

— English

It requires more courage not to fight than to fight.

— American

One man with courage is a majority.

— American

Courage/Cowardice

True courage is knowing how to suffer.

— Haitian

Courage is not the same as fighting someone
stronger than you.   — Swahili

A cowardly hyena lives longer.   — Tongan

Coward, strangle your fear, or else you will
strangle yourself.   — Ovambo

Better face a danger once than be always in fear.

— English

Courtesy

If you go to a rat's village and it is eating palm
nuts, you eat some too.   — Tshi

To salute a dwarf by bowing will not prevent you
from rising to your full height again.   — Hausan

If you ask for directions rudely, you may end up
twenty miles from your destination.
                                          — Chinese

Follow the good and learn their ways.
                                          — Chinese

The company of the wicked is like living in a fish
market; one becomes used to the foul odor.
                                          — Chinese

When you go to someone else's house and the
owner is squatting there on the ground, you do
not ask for a stool.   — Ashanti

Where flies are eaten, eat them.   — Ugandan

Full of courtesy, full of craft.   — English

Pluck not a courtesy in the bud.   — English

He that asketh a courtesy promiseth a kindness.
                                              — English

Courtesy is appropriate for gentlemen and
necessary for thieves.   — American

Courtesy is the password to safety.   — American

Courtesy on one side only never lasts for long.
                                              — American

Criticism

Criticism of the brave is behind his back.

— Igbo

If you laugh at the bowl, you laugh at the potter.

— Gandan

Do not belittle what you did not cultivate.

— Ugandan

Cuss-cuss never bore hole a man' kin.

— Jamaican

Whoever objects to the moon's position, let them climb up and adjust it.

— Hausan

To the white horse the zebra said: "I am white too," and to the black horse: "I am really black."

— Namibian

Faults and virtues are but two sides of the
same coin.   — Chinese

The hypocrite is known by his actions, not by
his clothes.   — Mexican

He who does not praise a thing is he who buys it.
                                        — Mexican

The barking of dogs does not reduce the beggar's
daily allotment.   — Arabic

No one says, "My yogurt is sour!"   — Arabic

To sit by the ring and tell the man inside, "Knock
him down!"   — Arabic

The garlic said to the onion: "You stink!"
                                        — Arabic

The sting of a reproach is the truth of it.
                                        — English

Woe to the house where there is no chiding.
                                        — English

Better a little chiding than a good deal of
heartache.   — English

When a man's coat is threadbare it is easy to pick
a hole in it.   — English

Criticism is something you can avoid by saying
nothing, doing nothing, and being nothing.
                                        — American

Death

Death don't see no difference 'tween the big house
and the cabin.   — African American

When an elephant is dead, a hare will not smell.
                                        — Fulani

The last to breathe is the first to drown.
El ultimo en banarse es el primero en ahogarse.
                                        — Costa Rican

Death and marriages make changes.
Éag is imirce a chloíos tíobhas.   — Irish

When death comes, it will not go away empty.
Nuair a thiocfas an bás ní imeoidh sé folamh.
                                        — Irish

Fame lives on after death.
Is buaine gladh ná saol. — Irish

Death is the poor man's doctor.
'Sé an bás leigheas an duine bhoicht. — Irish

Both your friend and your enemy think that you
will never die.
*Síleann do chara agus do namhaid nach bhfaighidh
tú bás choíche.* — Irish

Weep for the mourners, not for the dead; they
have gone to their rest, and we are left to lament.
*B'chu la'availeem v'lo la'aveda, shehu limnucha,
v'anu l'anacha.* — Hebrew

Death does not knock on the door.
— Yiddish

Immortality is surely a pleasant feeling, especially when the individual is still alive.

Almavet hu b'vadai reguesh na'eem m'od, b'yichud kol od ha'eesh chei. — Hebrew

When someone claims an inheritance, he sometimes has to pay for the funeral.

Az a mentsh kumt optzunemen die yerusha, darf er amol oich batzolen far die l'veiyeh.

— Yiddish

He is the sunshine at the edge of the roof.

— Arabic

Death is a camel which sleeps in everyone's house.

— Arabic

When a blind man dies, he is praised as having
beautiful eyes.   — Arabic

You can smell his halvah.   — Arabic

Death devours lambs as well as sheep.
                                   — English

There is but one road out of the Tower and that
leads to the scaffold.   — English

Death to the wolf is life to the lamb.
                                   — American

Death fiddles and we dance.   — American

Death & Life

At someone's funeral we weep for our own
mothers and fathers.
         — Tshi

I am not dead yet. I can suffer a bit more.
         — Namibian

She who keeps losing children doesn't invent
names anymore.
         — Ugandan

The burial ceremonies are quite bothersome when
the dead calls for more attention than when he
was alive.
         — Hayan

Those who die through ignorance are many; those
who die because they are intelligent are few.
         — Yoruban

He that lives most dies most.　　　— English

Live your own life, for you die your own death.
　　　　　　　　　　　　　　　— American

Debt

Do not run into debt with a rich man, or promise
anything to a poor one.　　　— Cuban

Clear accounts make for long friendships.
Cuentas claras, amistades largas.　　— Uruguayan

Pay what you owe and you will know what you
are worth.　　　　　　　　　— Mexican

Old debts are not paid, and new ones are left to
get old.
*Las deudas viejas no se pagan, y las nuevas se dejan
envejecer.*　　　　　　　　　— Mexican

He who has a hundred and one pesos, and owes a hundred and two, let him commend himself to God.

— Mexican

Clear accounts and thick chocolate.

— Argentinean

He who owes nothing has bought nothing on layaway.

El que nada debe nada ha adquirido a plazos.

— Cuban

A good borrower is a lazy payer.

— Russian

Creditors have better memories than debtors.

— Russian

A poor man's debt makes a great noise.

— English

There is never a debt is paid so high as that which the wet owes to the dry. — English

There is no benefit that sticks to the fingers. — English

Touch pot, touch penny. — English

Promise is debt. — English

You can run into debt, but you have to crawl out. — American

Rather than run into debt, wear your old coat. — American

Deception

When one dog barks for nothing, all other dogs
bark in earnest.

Ikken kyo ni hoete banken jitsu wo tsuto.

— Japanese

Business and folding screens must be crooked
to stand.

Shobai to byobu wa magaranu to tatanu.

— Japanese

That which covers thee discovers thee.

— English

He that cheateth in small things is a fool, but in
great things is a rogue. — English

What can't speak can't lie. — English

They that think no ill are soonest beguiled.

— English

Many a rose-cheeked apple is rotten at the core.
Is minic a bhios an tull dearg go hule ina chroi.

— Irish

The miller's pigs are fat but it wasn't all mouter
they ate.
*Bionn muca ma muilteoiri ramhar; ma ta, is ag Dia
ata a fhios ce leis an mhin a d'ith siad.* — Irish

If a man deceive me once, shame on him; but if
he deceive me twice, shame on me. — English

A shady lane breeds mud. — American

Watch out for wooden nickels. — American

Thieves hunt in couples, but a liar has no accomplice. — American

Deceit is a lie which wears a smile.

— American

Defeat & Victory

If your mind is strong, all difficult things will become easy; if your mind is weak, all easy things will become difficult. — Chinese

Occupy the higher ground to exercise control.

— Chinese

Defeat is never a bitter brew until one agrees to swallow it. — Chinese

Fight only when you can win; move away when you cannot. — Chinese

Defeat isn't bitter if you don't swallow it.

— American

Deity

The Great Spirit is not perfect: it has a good side and a bad side. Sometimes the bad side gives us more knowledge than the good side. — Lakota

When you lose the rhythm of the drumbeat of God, you are lost from the peace and rhythm of life. — Cheyenne

The rainbow is a sign from Him who is in all things. — Hopi

There is no god like the throat: it takes sacrifices daily. — Nigerian

God never sends mouths but He sends meat.

— English

The best way to see divine light is to put out your own candle.

— English

Where God builds a church, the devil will build a chapel.

— English

God comes at last when we think He is furthest off.

— English

The deities of one age are the bywords of the next.

— American

Look out for others and God will look out for you.

— American

Destiny

Every Ananya has his Melania.   — Russian

All roads lead to Moscow.   — Russian

You may grow taller, but no taller than your head.
     — Bassa

Destiny leads the willing but drags the unwilling.
     — American

Your whole destiny is involved in the attitude you
take toward your sin.   — American

Dilemma

It is difficult to throw a stone at a lizard that is
clinging to a pot.   — Ashanti

The goat says the sickness of its owner is causing it [to] worry. If the sickness worsens, the healer asks for a goat as [a] sacrifice. If the owner gets well, a goat is required to celebrate recovery.

— Yoruban

Who ha' fingernail no ha' itch, and who ha' itch no ha' fingernail. — Jamaican

There is weeping when separated, there is quarreling when together. — Swahili

It is easy enough to steal a fowl, but where are you going to eat it? — Hausan

Diligence

Gems are polished by rubbing, just as men are made brilliant by trials. — Chinese

Do not hope to reach a destination without leaving the shore. — Chinese

The one who removed the mountain was the one who began carrying away stones. — Chinese

Failure is not falling down but refusing to get up. — Chinese

Everyone is weary: the poor in seeking, the rich in keeping, the good in learning. — English

Discipline

Even when a samurai has not eaten, he holds his toothpick high.

Bushi wa kuwanedo taka-yoji. — Japanese

Though the wind blows, the mountain does not move.

Kaze fuke domo yama wa ugokazu. — Japanese

One word let slip and four horses would fail to catch it.

Ichigon wo izureba shiba mo oi-gatashi.

— Japanese

A single arrow is easily broken, but not ten in a bundle.

Ichijo no ya wa orubeku, jujo wa orubekarazu.

— Japanese

The bandits in the mountain are easily subjected, but it is difficult to subject the bandits in my heart.

Sanchu no zoku tairageru koto yasuku, shinchu no zoku tairageru koto katashi. — Japanese

A clever hawk hides its talons.
No aru taka wa tsume o kakusu. — Japanese

Discretion

A closed mouth catches no flies.
In bocca chiusa non entrano mosche. — Italian

If your head is wax, do not walk in the sun.
Chi ha il capo di cera, non vada al sole.
— Italian

Dirty clothes are washed in the backyard.
— Swahili

He who speaks too much is tiresome; he who
speaks too little is a bore.
*El que hable demás cansa y el que habla de
menos aburre.* — Mexican

You must not tell all that you know, nor judge all that you see, if you would live in peace.

— Mexican

He who talks too much errs much.

— Mexican

A word and a stone once thrown away cannot be returned.　　　— Mexican

Let not the tongue speak what the head may have to pay for.　　　— Mexican

Keep your counsel arrested until it's requested.
Guarda tu ayuda para quien te la pida.

— Mexican

He who spits in the air will have it fall back on his face.　　　— Mexican

The tongue slow and the eyes quick.

— Mexican

Empty not your soul to everybody and do not diminish thereby your importance.

— Ancient Egyptian

Guard your tongue in youth, and in age you may mature a thought that will be of service to your people.

— Sioux

Never help a person who doesn't help anybody else.

— Hopi

Thoughts are like arrows: once released, they strike their mark. Guard them well or one day you may be your own victim.

— Navajo

Discretion is the better part of valor.   — English

Do not spit into the well you may have to
drink of. — Russian

A close mouth catches nae fleas. — Scottish

Ale-sellers shouldna be tale-tellers. — Scottish

An ounce of discretion is worth a pound of wit.
— American

Diversity

It takes all kinds of trees to make a forest.
— Russian

It is at courts as it is in ponds; some fish,
some frogs. — English

Drink

Wha' a sober heart conceal a drunken tongue
reveal.   — Bajan

Godamighty mek man straight, a rum mek him
can't 'tan' up.   — Jamaican

Without wine, even beautiful cherry blossoms
have small attraction.
Saké nakute nan noonore ga sakura kana.
                                                       — Japanese

First the man takes a drink, then the drink takes
a drink, then the drink takes the man.
*Ippai wa hito sake o nomi, ni-hai wa sake sake
o nomi, sam-bai wa sake hito o nomu.*
                                                       — Japanese

As to flowers, when half open; as to saké, when a person is half tipsy.
Hana wa hankai, saké wa bisui. — Japanese

As you brew, so must you drink. — Russian

Coffee from the top of the cup and chocolate from the bottom. — Cuban

Intoxication is not the wine's fault but man's. — Russian

Dead with tea and dead without it.
Marbh le tae agus marbh gan e'. — Irish

The three faults of drinking are: a sorrowful morning, a dirty coat, and an empty pocket.
Tribhua an olachain: maidin bhronach, cota salach, pocai floamha. — Irish

When the wine is run out, you stop the leak.

— Russian

A full cup must be carried steadily.   — English

Wine sets an edge to wit.   — English

It is a good wind that blows a man to the wine.

— English

Bread is the staff of life, but beer's life itself.

— English

It is all right to drink like a fish if you drink what
a fish drinks.   — American

Drink like hell and be happy.   — American

Education

A learned man is twice born.　　　— Argentinean

The wise man never says, "I did not think."
　　　　　　　　　　　　　　　　— Cuban

Instruction in youth is like engraving in stones.
　　　　　　　　　　　　　　　— Colombian

One may study calligraphy at eighty.
Hachiju no tenarai.　　　　　　— Japanese

A full belly is not the stomach of a scholar.
Taishoku hara ni mitsureba gakumon hara ni irazu.
　　　　　　　　　　　　　　　— Japanese

A boy living near a Buddhist temple can learn an untaught sutra by heart.

Monzen no kozo narawanu kyo o yomu.

— Japanese

A person can study for seventy years and at the end die a fool.

A mentsh ken lernen zibitzig yor un tzum sof shtarben a nar.

— Yiddish

By learning you will teach; by teaching you will learn.

— English

Write with the learned, but speak with the vulgar.

— English

Education doesn't come by bumping your head against the school house.

— American

Education is the best provision for old age.
                                    — American

Never let your education interfere with your
intelligence.   — American

Effort

Hand plow can't make furrows by itself.
                                    — African American

Ain't no use askin' the cow to pour you a glass
of milk.   — African American

Talkin' 'bout fire doesn't boil the pot.
                                    — African American

The chakata fruit on the ground belongs to all,
but the one on the tree is for she who can climb.
                                    — Shona

Without stooping down for the mushroom, you cannot put it in your basket. — Russian

The third's the charm. — English

He that will have a cake out of the wheat must tarry the grinding. — English

God is better pleased with adverbs than with nouns. — English

Industry need not wish. — American

Paddle your own canoe. — American

Elders

Never see an old person going to carry water without getting a bucket and going in their stead.

— Twanas

When an elder speaks, be silent and listen.

— Mohawk

Old age is not as honorable as death, but most
people want it. — Crow

Cherish youth, but trust old age. — Pueblo

Never sit while your seniors stand. — Cree

Emotion

When the eyes see nothing, the heart feels
nothing.

Ojos que no ven, corazon que no siente.

— Panamanian

A man's heart and the autumnal sky.

Otoko-gokoro to aki no sora. — Japanese

A woman's heart and spring weather.
Onna na kokoro to haru-biyori. — Japanese

To change like the eyes of a cat.
Neko no me no yo ni kawaru. — Japanese

Jizo's face when borrowing; Emma's face when repaying.
Kariru toki no Jizo-gao, kaesu toki no Emma gao.
— Japanese

He flies into the flame, the summer insect.
Tonde hi ni iru natsu no mushi. — Japanese

Fire is love and water sorrow. — English

If the heart is right, the head cannot be very far wrong. — American

Endurance

Little by little the mouse finishes the hide.

— Sukuma

The quick one may not win; the enduring
one will. — Tswanan

Dip the pitcher into the water enough and it
finally breaks.
Tanto va el cantaro al agua, que por fin se quiebra.
— El Salvadoran

Gems are polished by rubbing, just as men are
made brilliant by trials. — Chinese

The tongue is soft but constantly remains; the
teeth are hard yet they fall out. — Chinese

Either do not begin or, having begun, do not give up. — Chinese

What can't be cured must be endured. — English

He that endures is not overcome. — English

A light burden's heavy if far borne. — English

First endure, then pity, then embrace. — American

Environment

A child brought up where there is always dancing cannot fail to dance. — Nyanjan

When a yam doesn't grow well, we don't blame it; it is because of the soil. — Tshi

Big fish do not live in small ponds.
Taigyo wa shochi ni sumazu. — Japanese

Monkeys must disperse once their tree falls.
— Chinese

What a man can be is born with him; what he becomes is a result of his environment.
— American

Envy

Envy shoots at others and wounds herself.
— Costa Rican

Let the dogs bark; it's a sign that we are galloping ahead.
Dejad que los perros ladren, es señal que cabalgamos.
— Spanish

Everyone stones the tree that bears fruit.
Al árbol que da frutos, toto el mundo lo apedrea.
— Mexican

Envy follows merit like the shadow follows
the body.
*La envidia sigue al mérito, como la sombra al
cuerpo.* — Nicaraguan

Hills far away are green but they often have
sour bottoms.
*Is glas iad na coic i bhfad uainn, Mas glasmhar iad,
ni fearmhar.* — Irish

Better to be envied than pitied. — English

The other side of the road always looks cleanest.
— English

All covet, all lose.   — English

The covetous spends more than the liberal.
          — English

As love thinks no evil, so envy speaks no good.
          — English

Envy is left-handed praise.   — American

A friend's envy is worse than an enemy's hatred.
          — American

Envy is destroyed by true friendship.
          — American

Envy doesn't enter an empty house.   — American

Equality/Superiority

A tree of your height cannot shade you.

— Swahili

He that does not fear a bull must be a bull
himself.   — Swahili

Nobleness is not noble ancestry.   — Swahili

The eagle does not catch flies.   — English

At the end of the game the king and the pawn go
into the same bag.   — English

Equality begins in the grave.   — American

Essence

The crow flew over the sea but returned still
a crow.   — Russian

A pig in a parlor is still a pig.   — Russian

Near is my shirt, but nearer is my skin.
                                           — Russian

One naturally prefers one's own kind.
                                           — Russian

Crows are black the world over.   — Russian

Evil

If you see wrongdoing or evil and say nothing
against it, you become its victim.   — African

People are consumed by evil because of keeping
close to it, but not because of keeping away
from it.   — Kikuyu

In order to find evildoers, every human being is
given a name.   — Tshi

Tald ob de debil an you heeh he wings.
                                            — Guyanan

Evil comes to us by ells and goes away by inches.
                                            — English

Welcome, evil, if thou comest alone.
                                            — English

Evil be to him who thinks it.   — English

Evildoers are evil dreaders.   — English

Small evils hatch quick.   — American

Desperate evils require desperate remedies.
     — American

Apprehension of evil is worse than the evil itself.
     — American

Bad to do evil, but worse to boast about it.
     — American

Experience

A satisfied person does not know what a hungry one feels.   — Fulani

A travelled child knows better than the old man who sits at home.   — Igbo

The macaco [*monkey*] doesn't climb up the
[*thorny*] acacia tree two times.   — Haitian

An old woman is not old in a song she
dances well.   — Nigerian

When the music stops, a deaf person continues
to dance.   — Igbo

He who does not go to sea knows not how
to pray.   — Ecuadoran

See and believe, and in order not to make a
mistake, touch.   — Colombian

Only he who carries it knows how much the
cross weighs.
Sólo sabe cuánto pesa la cruz, quien la va cargando.
          — Peruvian

The man who knows two languages is worth
two men.
Chi parla due lingue é doppio uomo.   — Italian

Experience without learning is better than
learning without experience.
*L'esperienza senza il sapere é meglio che il sapere
senza sapienza.*   — Italian

All things are difficult before they are easy.
Tutte le cose sono difficili prima di diventar facili.
                                          — Italian

The skill of using a mortar and pestle never
leaves one.
Mukashi totta kinezuka.   — Japanese

There are as many ways of making a living as
seeds of grass.
Shobai wa kusa no tane.   — Japanese

Calm seas make sorry sailors.
Mar tranquilo hace mal marino.   — Mexican

So many years playing the marquise and she still
doesn't know how to wave a fan.
*Tantos anos a la marquesa y no sabe menear el
abanico.*   — El Salvadoran

Only the pallbearers know the weight of the dead.
Sólo el que carga el cajón sabe lo que pesa el muerto.
                                         — Mexican

The best bullfighter is the one in the box seats.
El mejor torero es el de la barrera.   — Mexican

Talking about bulls is not the same as facing them in the ring.

No es lo mismo hablar de toros que estar en el redondel. — Mexican

Shoot a daw [*magpie*] and a crow, and soon you'll hit a falcon. — Russian

He that would learn to pray, let him go to sea. — Russian

Experience is the mistress of fools. — English

Good judgement comes from experience, and experience comes from poor judgement. — English

A thimbleful of experience is worth a tubful of knowledge. — American

A thorn of experience is worth a wilderness
of advice. — American

Experience is a comb which fate gives to a man
when his hair is all gone. — American

Wide experience makes for deep tolerance.
— American

Expression

To "Get out of my house!" or "What do you want
with my wife?" there is no answer.
— Bolivian

If a man lends an ear, it's because he, too, wants
to speak. — Argentinean

Silence was never written down. — Puerto Rican

The eyes have one language everywhere.
— English

Fairness

"Hit me but I must not hit you" is no game at all.
— Tshi

The peacemaker dies, while the fighters survive.
— Ugandan

The grass torch that burns a bad house, also burns a good one. — Gandan

Justice becomes injustice when it makes two wounds on a head which only deserves one.
— Kongo

For great ills, great remedies.
A grandes males grandes remedios. — Honduran

Fair exchange is no robbery. — English

Speak fair, think what you will. — American

Faith

Whoever prays loudly, it shows he has little faith.
Hamashmee'a kolo bitfilato, harai zeh miktannai amana. — Hebrew

Faith is not a whole series of axioms but a whole way of life.
Ha'emunah aina ma'arechet shel mishpateem elah derech shel chayeem. — Hebrew

Faith sees by the ears. — English

Pin not your faith on another's sleeve.

— English

Faith without works is dead. — English

A proof of faith is obedience. — American

Faith begins where reason stops. — American

Familiarity

A river drowns the one who can swim.

— Kikuyu

Every man know whe' him own house de leak.

— Jamaican

New broom sweep clean, but de ole broom know de corner. — Jamaican

The fish don't see the water.   — Haitian

Everyone knows where his own shoe pinches him.
      — Mexican

Everyone is master of their own fear.
Cada quien es dueño de su miedo.   — Mexican

A good man finds his native soil in every country.
      — Mexican

He that knows thee will never buy thee.
      — English

Old chains gall less than new.   — English

The man in boots does not know the man
in shoes.   — English

Familiarity breeds contempt.   — English

Family

He who abandons his family, God forsakes him.
                                        — Venezuelan

No matter if the child's born blind, as long as it doesn't beg.
No importa que nazca ciego con tal de que no mendigue.   — Honduran

The man to whom God gives no children, the devil gives nieces and nephews.   — Venezuelan

Favor your own first, then others.
Favorece a los tuyos primero luego a los ajenos.
                                        — Peruvian

A crooked top on a crooked kettle.
Nejiri-gama ni nejiri-buta. — Japanese

May you live up to one hundred years and I up to ninety-nine.
Omae hyaku made, washa kujuku made.
— Japanese

A bad wife is a poor harvest for sixty years.
Akusai wa rokuju nen no fusaku. — Japanese

Earthquakes, thunderbolts, fires, fathers.
Jishin, kaminari, kaji, oyaji. — Japanese

A faithful wife does not marry again.
Teifu wa ryofu ni mamiezu. — Japanese

Brides and mothers-in-law are like dogs
and monkeys.
Yome to shuto wa inu to saru. — Japanese

Children yoke parents to the past, present
and future.
Ko wa sangai no kubikase. — Japanese

Don't try to cover the stone with a quilt.
Ishi ni futon mo kiserarezu. — Japanese

"My mother is indeed the best baby carrier," says
the baby. — Ugandan

Adam was the luckiest of men: he had no
mother-in-law.
*Adam haya ham'ushar ba'anasheem: lo hayeta
lo chotenet.* — Hebrew

Till age six, your son is your master; until ten, he's your servant; until sixteen, a wonderful adviser; from then on, he's either your friend or your enemy.

Ad shnat hashisheet, bincha adon, l'cha; ad k'tze ha'aseereet eved; ad shesh-esrai yo'etz peleh hu l'cha; min hu v'hala ohavcha o son'echa. — Hebrew

Nobody's family can hang up the sign, "Nothing the matter here." — Chinese

If your son-in-law is good, you gained a son. If he is bad, you've lost a daugther.

Eem hechatan tov. nosaf l'cha ben, eem ra, ata m'abed gam bat. — Hebrew

A wise son makes his father happy; a foolish one grieves his mother.

Ben chacham y'samach av u'ven k'seel tugat imo.

— Hebrew

Since God could not be everywhere, he created mothers.

Elokeem aino yachol lihiyot b'chol makom, lachen bara imahot. — Hebrew

There's no rain without thunder, and no children born without pain.

Ain gueshem blee ra'ameem, v'ain laida blee chavaleem. — Hebrew

If I am in harmony with my family, that's success. — Ute

In twenty-four hours, a house can become a patriarch. — Seneca

Even in Paradise, living all alone would be Hell. — Seneca

Mony aunts, mony emes, mony kin, but
few friends.   — Scottish

He who has daughters is always a shepherd.
                                        — English

Every family has a goodness of mercy.
                                        — American

In a united family, happiness springs up of itself.
                                        — American

Every family has at least one black sheep.
                                        — American

If you act as good as you look, you'll never shame
your family.   — American

Family/Home

[*At*] whatever age a child gets a problem, at the same age she has to shoulder the responsibility.

— Igbo

Chip neber fly far from de block.

— Jamaican

Eat fam'bly bittle but no cut fam'bly 'tory.

— Jamaican

A child is an axe; when it cuts you, you still pick it up and put it on your shoulder.

— Bemba

Blood follow vein.

— Jamaican

The son of a zebra also has stripes.

— Sukuma

An ugly child of your own is more to you than a beautiful one belonging to your neighbor.

— Gandan

If you love other people's children, you will love your own even more.

— Swahili

The woman whose sons have died is richer than a barren woman.

— Kikuyu

Impatience with your brother is in the flesh, it doesn't reach the bone.

— Mamprussi

A mother is not to be compared with another person—she is incomparable.

— Mongoan

The mother is she who catches the knife by the blade.

— Tswana

Parents give birth to the body of their children, but not always to their characters.　　— Gandan

Jaybird don't rob his own nest.

　　　　　　　　　　　　— African American

Farming

From the king to the beggar, they all depend on the farm.　　　　　　　　　　— Irish

You should never stop the plough to kill a mouse.

　　　　　　　　　　　　— Irish

More grows in a tilled field than is sown in it.

　　　　　　　　　　　　— Irish

When all things spoke the potato said, "Set me warm, dig me warm, eat me warm, that's all I want."

　　　　　　　　　　　　— Irish

If the potato misses, Ireland's beaten.   — Irish

A good farmer is known by his crops.   — Irish

It is not the big farmers who reap all the harvest.
Ni hiad na fir mhora a gherras an fomhar uilig.
                                                              — Irish

Much bread grows in a winter night.
                                                              — English

The more furrows the more corn.   — English

He that sows trusts in God.   — English

It does not always rain when a pig squeals.
                                                              — American

A farmer on his knees is higher than a gentleman
on his legs.   — American

Fate

No plant comes to flower but to wither.
                              — Southern African

The animal that is coming [*fated*] to be killed does
not hear the hunter cough.   — Tshi

For everyone there is an appointed time.
                              — Ancient Egyptian

An elephant hunter usually gets killed by
an elephant.   — Swahili

A danger escaped is no guarantee for the future.
                              — Kikuyu

If fate throws a knife at you, there are two ways of catching it: by the blade or by the handle.

— Dominican Republic

That which is done at night appears in the day.

— Uruguayan

He who doesn't die on the battlefield slips in the bathtub.

— Uruguayan

He who would be a redeemer ends up crucified.
El que a redentor se mete termina crucificado.

— Venezuelan

What is fated to be yours will always return to you.

— Chinese

If heaven drops you a date, it must be received with an open mouth.

— Chinese

Bald-headed men are ready-made Buddhist priests.
— Chinese

Often one finds destiny just where one hides to avoid it.
— Chinese

Fate leads those who are willing but must push those who are not.
— Chinese

He that is born to be hanged shall never be drowned.
Chi é destinato alla forca non annega. — Italian

New lords, new laws.
Nuovo padrone, nuova legge. — Italian

The shade of the same tree, the flowing of the same stream.
Ichiju no kage, ichiga no nagare. — Japanese

Darkness lies one inch ahead.
Issun saki wa yami.   — Japanese

Karma and shadows follow one everywhere.
Inga to kageboshi wa tsuite mawaru.   — Japanese

Fate aids the courageous.
Un wa yusha o tasuku.   — Japanese

The flow of water and the future of human beings
are uncertain.
Mizu no nagare to hito no yukusue.   — Japanese

The world is the world for the world.
Tenka wa tenka no tenka.   — Japanese

That's how the world is: wolves kill sheep.
Minhago shel olam: A'eveem horgueem ha'ezeem.
                                          — Hebrew

If a person is fated to drown, he'll lose his life
even in a teaspoon of water.
*Oib a mentsh iz bashert tzu dertrinken veren, vet er
farleeren zein leben afeelu in a lefele vasser.*

— Yiddish

Freedom for the free and heaven for the saved.

— Russian

Accidents will happen in the best-regulated
families.

— Russian

Pull out the beak and the tail gets stuck, pull out
the tail and the beak gets stuck.

— Russian

Gnaw the bone which is fallen to thy lot.

— English

There is no flying from fate.

— English

The fates lead the willing man; an unwilling man
they drag. — American

Fate can be taken by the horns, like a goat, and
pushed in the right direction. — American

Faults

De bes a field mus' hab weed. — Jamaican

De higher monkey climb de more him expose.
— Jamaican

Everyone puts his fault on the times.
— English

Faults are thick where love is thin. — English

Wink at small faults unless you can cast the
first stone. — English

The first faults are theirs that commit them, the second theirs that permit them. — English

If thou seest ought amiss, mend it in thyself.
— English

A fault confessed is half-redressed. — American

Bad men excuse their faults, good men leave them.
— American

By others' faults wise men correct their own.
— American

Favor

The prince is never guilty in his father's court.
— Igbo

Favour will surely perish as life. — English

The son of the god of thunder does not die of
lightning.   — Ewe

Kissing goes by favour.   — English

A favor to come is better than a hundred received.
                                              — American

To favor the ill is to injure the good.
                                              — American

An ounce of favor goes farther than a pound
of justice.   — American

Fear

All fear has much imagination and little talent.
Todo miedo tiene mucha imaginación y poco talento.
                                              — Colombian

If you always fear misfortune, you'll miss out
on happiness.
Eem tachat mipnai ha'ason lo tir'eh et ha'osher.
— Hebrew

Some have been thought brave because they were
afraid to run away. — English

Our fear commonly meets us at the door by
which we think to run from it. — English

Fear lends wings. — English

All weapons of war cannot arm fear. — English

Love is full of busy fear. — English

Fear no man, and do justice to all men.
— American

We seldom fear what we can laugh at.

— American

Food & Drink

There is never wanting an excuse for drinking.

— Cuban

Hunger has no law; it's just hungry.
El hambre no tiene ley sino hambre. — Honduran

Drunkenness does not produce faults; it
discovers them. — Chinese

Better to drink the weak tea of a friend than the
sweet wine of an enemy. — Chinese

Drinks drown your sorrow, but your sorrow
returns the morning after. — Chinese

Those who take medicine and neglect their diet
waste the skill of the physician.   — Chinese

The best cure for drunkenness is to see a drunken
man while you are sober.   — Chinese

Talk doesn't fill the stomach.
Cha líontar an bolg le caint.   — Irish

Choose your company before you go drinking.
Toigh do chuideachta sula raghair ag ól.   — Irish

What won't choke will fatten and clean dirt is
no poison.   — Irish

Help is always welcome, except at the table.
Is maith an rud cúnamh, ach ag an mbord.

        — Irish

Long churning makes bad butter.
Maistreadh fada a níos an drochim. — Irish

You cannot sup soup with a fork.
*Níl ann ach seafóid a bheith ag ól anraithe
le forc.* — Irish

Drunkenness and anger speak truthfully.
Adeir siad go gcanann meisce nó fearg fíor.
— Irish

He who only drinks water does not get drunk.
An té a ólas ach uisce, cha bhíonn sé ar meisce.
— Irish

The wine is sweet, the paying bitter.
Is milis á ól ach is searbh á íoc é. — Irish

Good as drink is, it ends in thirst.
Dá fheabhas é an t-ól is é an tart a dheireadh.

— Irish

Hunger makes hard beans sweet.
La fame muta le fave in mandorle. — Italian

Wine is old men's milk.
Il vino é il latte dei vecchi. — Italian

In wine there is truth.
La veritá é nel vino. — Italian

A drunkard at prayer is regarded as an idol
worshipper.
Shikor shemitpalel k'eelu oved avoda zara.

— Hebrew

Wine renews the passion of lovers, and the hatred of enemies.

Hayayeen y'chadesh ahavat ha'ohev viy'orer et aivat ha'oyev. — Hebrew

Till age forty it is better to eat. After that, drinking is better.

Ad arba'een shnain maichla m'alai, mikan v'ailach mishtai m'alai. — Hebrew

To the hungry man no bread is bad.

— Mexican

There's no better sauce than a good appetite.

No hay mejor salsa que un buen apetito.

— Mexican

Man can adjust to anything except not eating.
A todo se acostumbra el hombre, menos a no comer.
— Mexican

To the satiated bird, cherries taste bitter.
— Mexican

A dreigh drink is better than a dreigh sermon.
— Scottish

He's like the smith's dog—so weel used to the
sparks that he'll no burn.   — Scottish

Death and drink-draining are near neighbors.
— Scottish

You hae been smelling the bung.
— Scottish

Good eating deserveth good drinking.

— English

Food/Hunger

Hungry belly and full belly neber walk one pass.

— Jamaican

If stars were loaves, many people would sleep out.

— Jamaican

One cannot borrow a man's mouth and eat onions
for him. — Fulani

If the lizard were good to eat, it would not be
so common. — Haitian

A full pig in the sty doesn't find the hungry one going by.

Ni aithnionn an mhuc a bhios sa chro an mhuc a bhios ag dul an rod. — Irish

Feed a cold and starve a fever. — English

"My belly thinks my throat is cut," as the hungry man said.

Sileann mo bholg go bhfuil mo scornach gearrtha. — Irish

An empty bag cannot stand upright. — English

Of soup and love, the first is best. — English

A dog returns to where he has been fed.

— American

Hunger finds no fault with moldy corn.

— American

More die of food than famine. — American

Fools & Folly

A leopard is chasing us and do you ask me: "Is it a
male or female?" — Temne

You don't study to be a fool.
Para tonto no se estudia. — Uruguayan

A warning to the wise is a blessing, to the fool
an insult. — Swahili

Do not argue with a fool, for people will not be
able to tell between the two of you. — Igbo

When a fool is told a proverb, it has to be explained to him. — Tshi

He who lacks ideas makes those of others his own.
El que carece de ideas hace suyas las ajenas.
— Puerto Rican

There's nothing worse for an intelligent person than to put a fool beside him. — Nicaraguan

If you return an ass's kick, most of the pain is yours. — Cuban

Learned fools are the greatest fools.
I pazzi per lettera sono i maggiori pazzi. — Italian

It is better to be a beggar than a fool.
Meglio mendicante che ignorante. — Italian

If the blind lead the blind, both fall into
the ditch.
*Se un cieco guida un altro cieco, ambedue cadono
nella fossa.* — Italian

Fools give parties, sensible people go to them.
Gli stolti fanno le feste e gli accorti se le godono.
— Italian

Even if a fool remains silent, he is considered wise.
Gam eveel machareesh, chacham yechashev.
— Hebrew

The worst kind of person is one whose power of
speech is greater than his power of thought.
*Hagaru'a bivnai adam hu mee sheco'ach l'shono oleh
al co'ach sichlo.* — Hebrew

The wise man's nakedness is between his loins,
and that of the fool between his cheeks.
*Ervat hachachameem bain raglaihem, v'ervat
hak'seel bain l'chayav.*   — Hebrew

Whoever hates a reprimand is stupid.
Soneh tochachat—ba'ar.   — Hebrew

The world is in the hands of fools.   — Hebrew

One needn't study to become a fool.
Para tonto no se estudia.   — Mexican

He who knows nothing neither doubts nor
fears anything.   — Mexican

It is better to be a fool than obstinate.
                                            — Mexican

There's no worse deaf man than the man who doesn't want to listen.

No hay peor sordo, que el que no quiere oír.

— Mexican

A fool may throw into a well a stone which a hundred wise men cannot pull out.   — Russian

One fisherman knows another from afar.

— Russian

Force a fool to pray and he'll crack his forehead.

— Russian

A fool is happier thinking weel o' himself than a wise man is of others thinking weel o' him.

— Scottish

The gravest fish is an oyster; the gravest bird's an ool; the gravest beast's an ass; and the gravest man's a fool. — Scottish

If I had a dog as daft as you I would shoot him. — Scottish

Fools make feasts and wise men eat them. — Russian

A gowk at Yule'll no be bright at Beltane. — Russian

Enjoy your little while the fool is seeking for more. — English

He who treats himself has a fool for a patient. — English

A fool at forty is a fool indeed.   — English

A fool's head never whitens.   — English

A fool will laugh when he is drowning.
                              — English

Fools build houses and wise men live in them.
                              — English

A fool can ask more questions in a minute than a
wise man can answer in an hour.   — American

A fool is like other men as long as he is silent.
                              — American

A fool talks most when he has the least to say.
                              — American

Foreigners

Beware of French people who pretend to quarrel with each other: they will join together to fight you.

— Malagasy

Learn fe dance at home before you go abroad.

— Jamaican

The white man has no kin. His kin is his money.

— Tsongan

When the white man is about to leave a garden for good, he wrecks it.

— Yoruban

If there had been no poverty in Europe, then the white man would not have come and spread his clothes in Africa.

— Tshi

Go abroad and you'll hear news of home.

— English

The Forest

Willows are weak but they bind other wood.

— Irish

If there is a way into the wood there is also a way out of it.

Ní lia bealach chun na coille ná bealach lena fágáil.

— Irish

Don't crow till you're out of the woods.

Ná tóg callán mór go bhfaighe tú amach as an choill.

— Irish

Bend with the tree that will bend with you.

Crom leis an chraobh a chromas leat. — Irish

Don't expect a cherry tree from an acorn.

— Irish

Some men go through a forest and see no firewood.
                                               — English

Fortune

Green maize abounds at the houses of those without teeth.
                                               — Shona

Han'some face and good luck don' trabble de same pass.
                                               — Jamaican

Some go out to fleece and come back sheared.
Hay quien va por lana y sale trasquilado.
                                               — Ecuadoran

Perhaps you will eat a whole elephant and nothing gets stuck in your throat, and then you eat a fish and a bone gets stuck in your throat.
                                               — Tshi

The lucky eagle kills a mouse that has eaten salt.
— Ugandan

It is better to eat bread with love than fowl
with grief.   — Bolivian

The favor of a man in power is like a
summer shower.   — Uruguayan

Fortune and olives are alike: sometimes a man has
an abundance and other times not any.
— Peruvian

A thrashing river is a fisherman's bounty.
En río revuelto, ganancia de pescadores.
— Bolivian

Luck and laziness go hand in hand.
Is minic a bhíos rath ar rapladh.   — Irish

Good luck beats early rising.
Es fearr an t-ádh maith ná éirí go moch.

It is not a matter of upper and lower class but of ups and downs.
Ní uasal ná iseal ach thuas seal agus thíos seal.

— Irish

Often have the likely failed and the unlikely prospered.
Minic a mheath dóigh is a tháinig andóigh.

— Irish

Better be sonsy than soon up.   — Scottish

Out o' the peat pot into the gutter.   — Scottish

Nae butter will stick to my bread.   — Scottish

Fortune aye favours the active and bauld.

— Scottish

Better rough an' sonsy than bare an' donsy.

— Scottish

Fortune favors the brave.   — Mexican

He who gets drenched at dawn has the rest of the
day to dry out.
El que temprano se moja tiempo tiene de secarse.

— Mexican

The ill-mannered child finds a father wherever
he goes.
El muchacho malcriado dondequiera encuentra padre.

— Mexican

How beautiful to watch the rain and not get wet.
Qué es ver llover y no mojarse. — Mexican

It's a bad start on the week for the man who is
hanged on a Monday.
*Mal comienza la semana aquel que es ahorcado
en lunes.* — Mexican

Misfortunes do not flourish on one path, they
grow everywhere. — Pawnee

Misfortunes will happen to the wisest and best
of men. — Pawnee

Elderberries in the yard and an uncle in Kiev.
— Russian

All the cones drop on poor Makar. — Russian

A lucky man can stumble upon a treasure while
an unlucky one can't even find a mushroom.
— Russian

There would be no good fortune had misfortune
not helped. — Russian

It's nice to have a spoon in time for dinner.
— Russian

God bestows no horns upon an ill-tempered cow.
— Russian

Your tongue will get you to Kiev. — Russian

Misfortunes come on wings and depart on foot.
— English

He dances well to whom fortune pipes.
— English

Friends

Heaps of good cotton stocks get chopped up from association with the weeds.

— African American

Tell me who your friends are and I'll tell you who you are. — Russian

Friendship is one thing and tobacco [*business*] is another. — Russian

Three faithful friends: an old wife, an old dog, and ready money. — American

Pretend you're in great danger, and you'll find out if you have any friends.
Fingete en gran peligro y sabias si tienes amigos.

— Nicaraguan

There is no better looking-glass than an
old friend.   — English

It's good to have some friends both in heaven
and hell.   — English

He quits his place well that leaves his friend there.
                                     — English

Live with your friend as if he might become
your enemy.   — English

When friends fall out the truth doth appear.
                                     — English

Friends tie their purse with a cobweb thread.
                                     — English

A benevolent man should allow a few faults in himself to keep his friends in countenance.

— American

A friend at hand is better than a relative at a distance.

— American

A friend won with a feather can be lost with a straw.

— American

It takes half your life to learn who your friends are and the other half to keep them.

— American

Friends & Enemies

Don't be like a shadow: a constant companion, but not a comrade.

— Malagasy

Better an intelligent enemy than a stupid friend.

— Swahili

Treat your guest as a guest for two days; on the
third day, give him a hoe.   — Swahili

Do not whirl a snake in the air when you have
killed it; the ones which remain in their holes
see you.   — Thongan

The enemy I know is better than the one I do
not know.   — Kikuyu

A false friend's tongue is sharper than a knife.
                                          — Argentinean

Jovial companions make this dull life tolerable.
                                          — Cuban

Cheese, wine, and a friend must be old to
be good.   — Cuban

There is no better mirror than the face of an
old friend.   — Cuban

A friendship that dies is never reborn.
Amistad que murió, nunca renace.   — Belizean

Renounce a friend who covers you with his wings
and destroys you with his beak.   — Nicaraguan

Eat the bread of the man you hate and also of him
you love.   — Puerto Rican

A good friend is better than a near relation.
                                        — Argentinean

It's easier to know your enemies than to know
your friends.
Es más fácil conocer al enemigo que al amigo.
                                             — Bolivian

He who has servants has unavoidable enemies.

— Puerto Rican

Don't be like the shadow: a constant companion,
yet not a comrade.   — Dominican Republic

Who's a hero? He who turns his enemy into
his friend.
Aizehu guibor? Ha'oseh son'o l'ohavo.   — Hebrew

If you see your friend's ox or sheep straying, don't
look the other way; return them to your friend.
*Lo tireh et shor acheecha o et seyo nidacheem
v'hitalamta mehem. Hashev t'sheevem l'acheecha.*
— Hebrew

My friend tells me of my virtue. My enemy notes
my fault.
*Ohavee yoranee yitronee, v'oyevee yodee'ainee
chesronee.*   — Hebrew

Whoever welcomes his friend with a smile, it's as though he gave his friend the finest gifts in the world.

Hamekabel et chavero b'sever paneem yafot, k'eelu natan lo kol matanot tovot sheba'olam.

— Hebrew

True friendship is one soul shared by two bodies.

La amistad sincera es un alma repartida en dos cuerpos.

— Mexican

Men meet, only mountains do not.

— Mexican

Trust your best friend as you would your worst enemy.

Desconfía de tu mejor amigo como de tu peor enemigo.

— Mexican

He who walks with wolves learns to howl.

El que con lobos anda a aullar se enseña.

— Mexican

He who never goes to your house doesn't want
you in his.

El que nunca va a tu casa en la suya no te quiere.

— Mexican

He who makes more of you than usual either
designs to cheat you or wants your assistance.

— Mexican

Only two relationships are possible—to be a
friend or to be an enemy.

— Cree

Don't walk behind me; I may not lead. Don't walk in front of me; I may not follow. Walk beside me that we may be as one. — Ute

A bold foe is better than a cowardly friend.
— Scottish

He that lends money to a friend has a double loss.
— Scottish

A drap and a bite's but a sma' requite.
— Scottish

A' are no friends that speak us fair. — Scottish

If you have no enemies it is a sign fortune has forgot you. — English

You may find your worst enemy or best friend
in yourself.   — English

No worst pestilence than a familiar enemy.
                                          — English

A reconciled friend is a double enemy.
                                          — American

False friends are worse than open enemies.
                                          — American

To have a friend, close one eye; to keep him,
close both.   — American

Friendship

If you want to know someone's character, look at the friends he keeps. — Chinese

Friendship between gentlemen appears indifferent but is pure like water. — Chinese

There is more friendship in a half pint of whiskey than in a churn of buttermilk.

Is mó an carthanas a bhíos i ngloine biotáille ná bhíos i mbairille bláthaí. — Irish

Friends are like fiddle-strings and they must not be screwed too tightly. — Irish

Don't be hard and don't be soft and don't desert your friend for your own share.

Ná bí cruaidh agus ná bí bog; ná tréig go charaid ar do chuid. — Irish

A friend's eye is a good mirror.
Is maith an scáthan súil carad. — Irish

No war is more bitter than the war of friends, but it does not last long.
Níl cogadh is géire ná cogadh na gcarad, ach ní bhíonn sé buan. — Irish

A kind word never broke anyone's mouth.
Níor bhris focal maith fiacail riamh. — Irish

There is no need like the lack of a friend.
Ní easpa go díth carad. — Irish

When a friend asks, there is no tomorrow.
Quando un amico chiede, non v'é domani.
— Italian

One enemy is too much for a man, and a hundred friends too few.

Un nemico é troppo, cento amici non bastano.

— Italian

You can live without a brother but not without a friend.

Si puó vivere senza fratelli ma non senza amici.

— Italian

There are formalities between the closest of friends.

Shitashiki naka ni mo reigi ari. — Japanese

The intimacy of water and fish.

Suigyo no majiwari. — Japanese

A hedge between keeps friendship green.

— German

Futility

To pound water with a mortar is futile.

— Kikuyu

A Buddha made of mud crossing a river cannot protect even himself.   — Chinese

When the itch is inside the boot, scratching outside provides little consolation.   — Chinese

Mass is not repeated for the deaf.   — Russian

One doesn't bring samovars to Tula.   — Russian

Cry not for the hair when the head is off.

— Russian

Carrying saut to Dysart and puddings to Tranent.

— Scottish

Pigs may whistle, but thay hae an ill mouth for't.
— Scottish

It's ill to take the breeks off a Hielandman.
— Scottish

A mill cannot grind with water that is past.
— American

You cannot drive a windmill with a pair of bellows.
— American

You cannot squeeze blood out of a stone.
— American

Generosity

Rather ten thousand lanterns from a wealthy man
than one lantern from a poor man.
Choja no mando, hinja no itto. — Japanese

A padded jacket is an acceptable gift even in
summer.
Itadaku mono wa natsu de mo kosode.
— Japanese

The generous man pays for nothing so much as
what is given him. — English

What bread men break is broken to them again.
— English

True generosity is the ability to accept ingratitude.
— American

The generous can forget that they have given, but the grateful can never forget that they have received. — American

Giving & Receiving

Gifts break rocks and melt hearts.
— Uruguayan

To give in order to receive is not to give, but to beg.
Dar para recibir, no es dar, sino pedir.
— Costa Rican

For the ugly vice of begging, there's the virtue of not giving.
Contra el feo vicio de pedir existe la virtud de no dar. — Venezuelan

He who gives charity anonymously is greater
than Moses.
Gadol ha'oseh tzedaka baseter yoter mimoshe
rabbenu. — Hebrew

If you want to control your soul, hand it as a gift
to your intellect.
Eem toveh limshol b'naf'sh'cha, t'na ota b'matana
l'sichl'cha. — Hebrew

Earth produces all things and recieves all again.
— English

The hand that gives gathers. — English

The charitable give out at the door and God puts
in at the window. — English

Let him who gives nothing be silent, and him
who recieves speak. — American

Who pleasure gives shall joy recieve.
— American

God/Religion

God has only one measure for all people.
— Haitian

A person looks only on the outside of things; God
looks into the very heart. — Efik

Prayer from de mout' alone is no prayer.
— Jamaican

The very thing you do not want, that is what
pleases God. — Swahili

It is God who cures, and the physician gets
the money.   — Chilean

The friar who prays in God's name prays for two.
Fraile que pide por Dios, pide para dos.
                              — Spanish

The little birds have God for their caterer.
                              — Chilean

God made us and we wonder at it.   — Cuban

Even a leaf does not flutter on the tree without
the will of God.   — Cuban

The mills of God grind slowly, yet they grind
exceedingly small.
Il mulino di Dio macina piano ma sottile.
                              — Italian

There's no going to heaven in a sedan.
In paradiso non ci va in carrozza. — Italian

God comes with leaden feet but strikes with
iron hands. — Russian

When God will punish, he will first take away the
understanding. — Russian

I would rather be your Bible than your horse.
— Scottish

God fits the back for the burden.
Chruthaight Dia an droim i gcomhair an ualaigh.
— Irish

Danger past, God forgotten. — Scottish

God keep ill gear out o' my hands; for if my hand
ance get it, my heart winna part wi't, sae prayed
the gude Earl of Eglinton.   — Scottish

Think and thank God.   — English

The nest of the blind bird is made by God.
                                      — English

God gives His anger by weight, but His pity
without measure.   — English

Trust in God but lock your car.   — American

It is not well for a man to pray cream and live
skim milk.   — American

Good & Evil

The devil always paints himself black, but we always see him rose-colored.

— Dominican Republic

He who walks the path of evil comes upon an evil end.

El que mal anda, mal acaba. — Honduran

There's nobody can prevent you getting into heaven, but there are many always ready to give you a shove into hell. — Nicaraguan

There is not the thickness of a peso between good and evil. — Puerto Rican

Good comes from far away; evil is close at hand.

El vien de lejos viene y el mal cerca lo tienes.

— Bolivian

A wicked man's gift has a touch of his master.
Il dono del cattivo é simile al suo padrone.

— Italian

A solitary man is either a beast or an angel.
Uomo solitario, o angelo o demone.   — Italian

There is no vice that does not occasionally have
some benefit, and no virtue that at times is not
hurtful to some people.
*Ain mida m'guna shelo tihiyeh to'elet—ma
bizmaneem m'suyameem, k'shem she'ain mida
m'shubachat she'ain la nezek bizmaneem rabeem.*

— Hebrew

Three rebel against the light: the thief, the
adulterer, and the bat.
Shlosha hema b'mordai ha'or: ganav, no'ef, v'atalef.

— Hebrew

Put another way, Satan is a person's wish to
do evil.

Hu satan, hu yetzer hara. — Hebrew

We should bolster the light rather than fight
the darkness.

*Tzazreech l'hagbeer et ha'or tachat l'hilachem
bachoshech.* — Hebrew

A stupidly devout man, the slyly evil, and the
sanctimonious woman—these will destroy
the world.

*Chaseed shoteh v'rasha arum v'eesha prusha: harai
elu m'chalai olam.* — Hebrew

The sleep of the wicked people is a benefit for
them and a boon to the world.

Shena lar'sha'eem hana'a lahem, v'hana'a la'olam.
— Hebrew

There is not the thickness of a sixpence between
good and evil.   — English

As there is guilt in innocence, there is innocence
in guilt.   — Yoruban

He who suffers many evils is comforted with just
a little good.
El que mucho mal padece con poco bien se conforma.
                                         — Mexican

With poison, one drop is enough.
De veneno, basta una sola gota.   — Mexican

Evil falls on him who goes to seek it.
                                         — Mexican

Once the dog's dead, the rabies end.
Muerto el perro, se acabó la rabia.   — Mexican

Gossip

He who says what he likes shall hear what he does not like.

Chi dice quel che vuole, ode quel che non vorrebbe.
— Italian

You surround your vineyard with thorns—place doors and locks on your mouth.   — Italian

Gossip is more horrible than a capital crime.
— Hebrew

Fire dies for lack of wood; if there's no whispering, gossip stops.

B'efes etzeem tichbeh esh, u'v'ain guirgan yishtok madon.   — Hebrew

Good deeds never leave home, bad ones echo a thousand miles. — Chinese

Base terms are bellows to a slackening fire. — English

If you make songs about yourself, you can't blame other people for singing them. — English

Whoever gossips to you will gossip of you. — American

Gossip/Lies

The slanderer kills a thousand times; the assassin but once. — Ecuadoran

Even the powerful ox has no defense against flies. — Chinese

True words may not be pleasant, pleasant words may not be true.   — Chinese

A lie has no legs, but a scandal has wings.
                                        — English

One seldom meets a lonely lie.   — American

You can get far with a lie, but not come back.
                                        — American

Gossip/Rumor

Listen to what they say of others and you will know what they say of you.   — Cuban

A hatchet in the mouth is more harmful than a hatchet in the hand.
Hace más daño un hacha en la boca que en la mano.
                                        — Paraguayan

A bad rumor is better than bad news.
Es mejor un mal rumor que una mala noticia.

— Chilean

That which is said at the table should be wrapped
up in the tablecloth. — Guatemalan

The dog that fetches will carry. — English

Anyone can start a rumor, but none can stop one.

— American

If you can't say something good about someone,
come sit right here by me. — American

Gratitude

Gratitude is the least of virtues; ingratitude is the worst of vices.   — Paraguayan

A favor given to man is appreciated by none.
Favor hecho a muchos no lo agradece ninguno.
                                                   — Nicaraguan

If God does not grant you glory, be content with fame.
Si Dios no te da gloria, confórmate con la fama.
                                                   — Brazilian

Never give thanks for a favor held back.
Favor retenido no debe ser agradecido.
                                                   — Chilean

Let every man praise the bridge he goes over.
                                                   — English

If every bird take back its own feathers, you'll
be naked. — English

He that gives to a grateful man puts out to usury.
— English

Never quarrel with one's bread and butter.
— American

Greed

There is no greater calamity than being consumed
by greed. — Chinese

Fat fries and burns itself. — Chinese

Our needs are few but our wants increase with our
possessions. — Chinese

They prevent us from getting red clay from the
pit, and they do not use it.　　　　　　— Xhosa

Buy what you have no need of and ere long you
shall sell your necessaries.
*Chi compra il superfluo, si prepara a vendere il
necessario.*　　　　　　　　　　　— Italian

Poverty wants many things, and avarice all.
*La povertá é priva di molte cose, l'avarizia é priva
di tutto.*　　　　　　　　　　　　— Italian

Who has land, has war.
Chi ha terra, ha guerra.　　　　　　— Italian

He who grabs much grasps little.
El que mucho abarca, poco aprieta.　　— Mexican

He who wants everything will lose everything.
Quien todo lo quiere todo lo pierde.

— Mexican

In the matter of pigs, all is money, and in the
matter of money, all are pigs.
*En cuestión de puercos todo es dinero, y en cuestión
de dinero todos son puercos.* — Mexican

Avarice commonly occasions injury to the person
who displays it. — Mexican

The fewer the donkeys, the more ears of corn.
Cuando menos burros, más olotes. — Mexican

If it were not for the belly, the back might
wear gold. — English

The more you eat, the more you want.

         — American

If you desire many things, many things will seem
but a few.   — American

Greed/Envy

Do not drink water in the house of a merchant:
he will charge you for it. — Ancient Egyptian

A tree belonging to an avaricious man bore
abundantly; but instead of gathering the fruit little
by little, he took an axe and cut it down that he
might get all at once.   — Yoruban

A greedy mek fly follow coffin go a hole.

         — Jamaican

Guile

A cunning man likes the company of a fool.

— Kikuyu

If you are too smart to pay the doctor, you had better be too smart to get sick. — Tswana

If you sell a drum in your own village, you get the money and keep the sound. — Malagasy

Happiness

Being happy in life is better than being a king.

— Hausan

Happiness requires something to do, something to love and something to hope for. — Swahili

If a man is unhappy, his conduct is the cause.

— Tshi

Wine, women and food give gladness to the heart.
— Ancient Egyptian

The place where you are happy is better than the place you were born.
— Tshi

Kittens are a child's instrument for happiness.
— Cuban

From the tree of silence hangs the fruit of tranquility.
— Peruvian

Every time one laughs a nail is removed from one's coffin.
— Honduran

Grief shared is half grief; joy shared is double joy.
— Honduran

Solitude is enjoyed only when one is at peace with
oneself.   — Chinese

When joy is extreme, it is the forerunner of grief.
                                                — Chinese

He is happy that knows not himself to be
otherwise.
Felice non é, chi d'esserlo non sa.   — Italian

Better to live well than long.
Meglio vivere ben che vivere a lungo   — Italian

He that has time, has life.
Chi ha tempo, ha vita.   — Italian

The best way to find happiness is not to search for it.

Haderech hatova b'yoter l'hasagat ha'osher hee shelo l'chapes oto. — Hebrew

If I am not for myself, who will be? But if I am only for myself, what am I? And if not now, then when?

Eem ain anee lee mee lee? U'ch'she'anee l'atzmee, ma anee? V'eem lo achshav, aimatei? — Hebrew

There is one moral duty that moralists underrate almost criminally—the duty to enjoy God's world.

Yesh chova musareet chat, shedavka hamusaraneem m'zalz'leem ba, ad k'dai avon pleelee—hachova lehanot me'olamo shel hakadosh baruch hu.

— Hebrew

If you can't find peace within you, you'll labor in vain to find it elsewhere.

Eem lo timtza hashalom b'kirb'cha, shav ta'amol l'matzehu b'makom acher. — Hebrew

All time spent angry is time lost being happy.

Todo el rato que está enojado, pierde de estar contento. — Mexican

He who lives with hope dies happy.

Quien con la esperanza vive, alegre muere. — Mexican

A man without happiness is either not good or not well.

Un hombre sin alegría no es bueno o no está bueno. — Mexican

Don't be afraid to cry. It will free your mind of sorrowful thoughts. — Hopi

Inner peace and love are the greatest of God's gifts. — Tenton Sioux

When we understand deeply in our hearts, we will fear and love and know the Great Spirit. — Oglala Sioux

The woman had no problems so she bought some pigs. — Russian

Living mindlessly is paradise. — Russian

A soldier on furlough lets his shirt hang out of his trousers. — Russian

You can't have two forenoons in the same day.

— Russian

There is an hour wherein a man might be happy
all his life, could he find it.   — English

Happy is the country which has no history.

— English

Joy was born a twin.   — English

If you would be happy for a week, take a wife; if
you would be happy for a month, kill a pig; but if
you would be happy all your life, plant a garden.

— English

Happy is the bride the sun shines on.   — English

Always to court and never to wed is the happiest
life that ever was led.   — English

Happiness multiplies as we divide it with others.
                                          — American

Happiness is a form of courage.   — American

The happiest place in the world to live is within
one's income.   — American

Real happiness is found not in doing the things
you like to do, but in liking the things you have
to do.   — American

Getting what you go after is called success, but
liking it while you are getting it is called
happiness.   — American

Health

For a rash to heal, you must stop scratching it.

— Sukuma

A man with a cough cannot conceal himself.

— Yoruban

If you have no time to take care of your sickness, you get time to die.

— Tshi

If you don't walk after eating, your food remains undigested.

— Hebrew

Sleep is better than medicine.

— Irish

A glutton lives to eat, a wise man eats to live.

— Irish

A good laugh and a long sleep are the two best
cures in the doctor's book.
Gáire maith is codladh fada—an dá leigheas is fearr
i leabhar an dochtúra. — Irish

What butter or whiskey will not cure is incurable.
An rud nach leigheasann im ná uisce beatha, níl
leigheas air. — Irish

Whiskey when you're sick makes you well;
whiskey makes you sick when you're well.
— Irish

The wearer best knows where the shoe pinches.
Ag duine féin is fearr fios cá luíonn a bhóg air.
— Irish

A light heart lives long.
Maireann croí éadrom i bhfad. — Irish

A person's health is in his feet.
I gcosa duine a bhíos a shláinte. — Irish

A heavy heart seldom combs a gray beard.
Cha chíorann tú ceann liath choíche. — Irish

It is better to lose health like a spendthrift than to hoard it like a miser. — English

Whatsoever was the father of the disease, an ill diet was the mother. — English

Medicines be not meat to live by. — English

Eat leeks in March, garlic in May, all the rest of the year the doctors may play. — English

It is easy for a man in health to preach patience to the sick. — American

Folks spend their health to acquire wealth and later spend their wealth to regain their health.

— American

Hearth & Home

Keep your house and your house will keep you.
Coinnigh do shiopa is coinneoidh do shiopa thú.

— Irish

There's no hearthstone like your own hearthstone.
Níl aon teallach mar do theallach féin. — Irish

When everybody's house is on fire go home and look at your own chimney.
Nuair atá teach do chomharsan le thine tabhair aire do do theach féin. — Irish

There is no place like home.
Níl aon tinteán mar do thinteán féin. — Irish

A house divided will soon fall.
Nuair bhíos daoine i bpáirt bíonn cuid ar leith
is coimhlint. — Irish

A man lives long in his native place.
Buan fear ina dhúiche. — Irish

A new broom sweeps clean, but the old one
knows the corners best.
Scuabann scuab úr go glan, ach tá fios ag an
seanscuab ar na coirnéil. — Irish

When thrown into the sea the stone said, "After
all, this is also a home." — Ugandan

A house built by the wayside is either too high
or too low. — English

The first year let your house to your enemy; the second to your friend; the third live in it yourself.

— English

Burn not your house to scare away the mice.

— English

You will never find a cat on a cold hearth.

— American

You can go home when you can go nowhere else.

— American

A house without books is like a room without windows.

— American

You can build a house but you must make a home.

— American

Night brings the cows home.   — American

Help

Ask help from the spirits after having used all
your strength.   — Ugandan

Help me during the floods, I will help you during
the drought.   — Hayan

Help you to salt. Help you to sorrow.
                                    — Italian

He that is fallen cannot help him that is down.
                                    — English

He helps little that helps not himself.   — English

God helps those who help themselves.
                                    — American

Slow help is no help.   — American

If you can't help, don't hinder.   — American

Self-help is the best help.   — American

A little help is worth a lot of pity.   — American

Home & Family

Govern a family as you would cook a fish—
very gently.   — Chinese

Who has children cannot long remain poor; who
has none cannot long remain rich.   — Chinese

When buying a house, check the beams; when
choosing a wife, check the mother.   — Chinese

The state of a nation is reflected in the home.
— Chinese

The gem of the sky is the sun; the gem of the house is the child.
— Chinese

You can't be the head of a family unless you show yourself both stupid and deaf.
— Chinese

If you want your children to have a quiet life, let them always be a little hungry and cold.
— Chinese

He that has no fools, knaves, or beggars in his family was begot by a flash of lightning.
— English

Home is home, though it be never so homely.
— English

Home is not a structure, but something in
your heart.   — American

Home is the father's kingdom, the children's
paradise, the mother's world.   — American

The longest mile is the last mile home.
                                               — American

Men build houses; women build homes.
                                               — American

A house is not a home.   — American

Honesty

If your child is dancing clumsily, tell him: "You
are dancing clumsily"; do not tell him: "Darling,
do as you please."   — Twi

She who doesn't say it to you isn't your friend.

— Ndongan

Every man honest till de day him ketch.

— Jamaican

That which the ear has heard, and the eye has seen, it is useless for your mouth to deny.

— Mongoan

The remedy for "don't let it be heard" is "don't let it be done."

— Hausan

I would rather be deceived by an intelligent person than by a jackass.

— Haitian

People are the thing: if I call "Gold," gold does not respond; if I call "Clothes," clothes do not respond; people are the thing.

— Twi

He who tells the truth doesn't sin, but he causes
many inconveniences. — Cuban

He who excuses himself, accuses himself.
Quien se excusa, se acusa. — Puerto Rican

The best of hunters lies more than he hunts.
El mejor cazador miente más que caza.
— Cuban

Clean hands offend no one.
Manos blancas no ofenden. — Colombian

Return property to its owner, and your sleep will
be peaceful.
Vuélvase lo suyo a su dueño, ye tendrás buen sueño.
— Guatemalan

Little thieves are hanged, great ones are honored.
*A rubar poco si va in galera, a rubar tanto si
fa carriera.* — Italian

He who holds a ladder is as bad as the thief.
Chi tiene la scala non é meno reo del ladro.
— Italian

A traveler may lie with authority.
Ha bel mentir chi vien da lontano. — Italian

Like a Buddha met with in hell.
Jigoku de hotoke ni au yo. — Japanese

Eggs and vows are easily broken.
Tamago to chikai wa kudake-yasui. — Japanese

To make the tea cloudy.
O-cha wo nigosu. — Japanese

When a bribe enters through the front door,
honesty departs through the window.
*B'heekanes hashochad derech hapetach, yivrach
hayosher derech hachalon.*   — Hebrew

Teach your tongue to say, "I don't know," rather
than invent something.   — Hebrew

When swindlers meet a genuinely honest man,
they're so astonished they regard him as a greater
swindler than themselves.
*K'sherama'eem nitkaleem b'adam yashar b'hechlet,
hem merov hafta'a choshveem oto l'ramr'ee gadol
mehem.*   — Hebrew

A slanderer kills three: himself, his listener, and
the person who was slandered.
*Ha'omer l'shon hara hu horeg shlosha: hamesapro,
hamekablo u'mee shene'emar alav.*   — Hebrew

A liar's punishment: even when he tells the truth,
people don't believe him.
*Cach onsho shel bada'ee: afeelu amar emet, ain
shom'een lo.* — Hebrew

An answer without a question signals guilt
without question.
Contestación sin pregunta, señal de culpa.
— Mexican

He who does not intend to pay is not troubled in
making his bargain. — Mexican

The dog that has his bitch in town never
barks well. — Mexican

The bowman who is a bad marksman has a
lie ready. — Mexican

Life is both giving and receiving.   — Mohawk

He who is present at a wrongdoing and does not
lift a hand to prevent it is as guilty as the
wrongdoers.   — Omaha

A liar can go round the world but cannot
come back.   — Russian

An ill-paying job is better than a lucrative heist.
                               — Russian

A fu' heart never lied.   — Scottish

It's a far cry to Loch Awe.   — Scottish

Truth and honesty keep the crown o' the causey.
                               — Scottish

You cannot make people honest by an Act
of Parliament.   — English

Beauty and honesty seldom agree.   — English

Honesty is praised and left to starve.
                                                  — American

An honest citizen is an exile in his own country.
                                                  — American

Honor

Only fools seek credit from the achievements of
their ancestors.   — Chinese

When a leopard dies, he leaves his coat. When a
man dies, he leaves his name.   — Chinese

A clear conscience is the greatest armor.

— Chinese

To scrape the light off one's face.   — Chinese

A man must despise himself before others will.

— Chinese

If you are honored, honor yourself.   — Twi

Honor a child and he will honor you.   — Ila

Although dying of thirst, I drink not the water of a stolen fountain.

Kasshi temo tosen no mizu wo nomazu.

— Japanese

Looking up we are not ashamed in the presence of heaven, nor bowing down are we ashamed in the presence of Earth.

Aoide ten ni hajizu, fushite chi ni hajizu.

— Japanese

He who steals incense smells of it.

Ko o nusumu mono wa ko ni arawaru.

— Japanese

The cherry blossom among flowers, the warrior among men.

Hana wa sakura, hito wa bushi.　　　— Japanese

If the fountainhead is clear, the stream will be clear.

Minamoto kiyokeraba nagare kiyoshi.

— Japanese

A tiger dies and leaves his skin; a man dies and leaves his name.

Tora wa shi shite kawa wo todome, hito wa shi shite na wo nokosu. — Japanese

Mountains are not esteemed because they are high, but because they have trees.

Yama takaki ga yue ni tattokarazu, ki aru wo motte tattoshi to nasu. — Japanese

No revenge is more honorable than the one not taken. — English

Honour follows those who flee from it. — English

Honour buys no beef. — English

There is honour among thieves. — English

The post of honour is the post of danger.

— English

A gracious woman obtains honor, and strong men obtain riches.

— American

Before honor is humility.

— American

Some are born to honor, and some have honor thrust upon them.

— American

Hospitality

A guest who comes empty handed does not deserve a warm welcome.

Ore'ach she'ba b'yadayeem raikot aino zocheh l'varuch haba.

— Hebrew

Men like guests more than women do.

— Hebrew

Being hospitable is more important than attending synagogue service early in the morning.
G'dola hachnasat orcheen yoter mehash'camat beit hakneset. — Hebrew

Come seldom, come welcome.
Ni bhionnfailte roimh minic a thig. — Irish

It is a sin against hospitality to open the doors and shut up the countenance. — English

Small cheer and great welcome make a great feast. — English

A merry host makes merry guests. — English

The fairer the hostess the fouler the reckoning. — English

Don't reckon with your host.   — English

Humanity

Man is like a breath, his days like a passing shadow.
Adam lahevel dama, yamav c'tzel over.
                                                 — Hebrew

Man has succeeded in overcoming tremendous spaces, but not the distance between one man and another.
Ha'adam hitzlee'ach l'hitgaber al merchakeem atzumeem v'al hamerchak bain adam l'chavero lo hitzlee'ach l'hitgaber.   — Hebrew

There are all kinds of people in the world: asses and mules, dogs and hogs, and also worms.
Yesh kol meenai bree'ot ba'olam: chamoreem u'fradot, klaveem v'chazeereem, v'gam tola'eem.   — Hebrew

God made man upright, but man searched out
many crooked devices.
*Elokeem asa et ha'adam yashar, v'hema bikshu
chishvonot rabeem.* — Hebrew

One man differs from another in three things: his
voice, his appearance, and his mind.
*Bishlosha d'vareem adam mishtaneh mechavero:
b'kol, b'mar'eh, u'v'da'at.* — Hebrew

There are no bad beasts except man.
Ain chayot ra'ot, p'rat l'achat-ha'adam.

— Hebrew

We are all Adam's children.
Tutti siamo figli di Adamo ed Eva. — Italian

People get the government they deserve.
Ogni popolo ha il governo che si merita. — Italian

Life is half spent before we know what it is.
La vita é giá mezzo trascorsa anziché si sappia che
cosa sia.   — Italian

Of doctor and poet, musician and madman, we
each have a trace.
De médico, poeta, músico y loco todos tenemos
un poco.   — Mexican

The dead to his burial ground, and the living to
his fooling around.
El muerto a la sepultura, y el vivo a la travesura.
      — Mexican

Everyone is as God made him and very often worse.
      — Mexican

He who is a parrot is green wherever he is.
El que es perico, dondequierra es verde.
— Mexican

There is hope from the sea but there is no hope
from the land.
Bionn suil le muit ach ni bhionn suil le tir.
— Irish

To err is human, to forgive divine.   — English

As a man lives, so shall he die.   — English

When you live next to the cemetery, you cannot
weep for everyone.   — English

A human learns how to talk early, but how to
keep silent late.   — American

We are as big as the thing which bothers us.

— American

Every man is occasionally what he ought to
be perpetually.   — American

Man changes often but improves seldom.

— American

Above all nations is humanity.   — American

Humor

Man strives, and God laughs.   — Yiddish

The more money, the happier; the more wit,
the happier.
*K'rov kaspo ya'asheer eesh, v'ach k'rov t'vunato
y'ushar.*   — Hebrew

Humor is an important asset: it means understanding and self-criticism. Where humor is absent, you'll find small-mindedness.

G'dola midat hahumor sheprusha gam havanat atzmo u'vikoret atzmo . . . kol makom she'ata motzeh he'der humor, ata motzeh katnut hamocheen.
— Hebrew

Everything is funny as long as it happens to someone else. — Russian

One is received according to one's dress and sent off according to one's wit. — Russian

He that laughs when he is alone will make sport in company. — English

Laugh before breakfast and you'll cry before lunch. — English

Laugh till you cry, sorrow till you die.

— English

Wit is more often a shield than a lance.

— English

He who laughs at others' woes finds few friends
and many foes. — American

Let them laugh that win. — American

A ripple of laughter is worth a flood of tears.

— American

Hunting & Fishing

If you are merciful to the antelope, you go to
bed hungry. — Tshi

"So near and yet so far," said the man when the bird lit on his gun.   — Irish

The wise bird flies lowest.   — Irish

It is hard to hunt the hare out of the bush it is not in.
Is doiligh an gearria a chur as an tomóg nach bhfuil sé ann.   — Irish

Praise the sea but keep near land.
Mol an mhónaidh is seachain í; cáin an choill is tathaigh í.   — Irish

Listen to the sound of the river and you will catch a trout.
Éist le tuile na habhann is gheobhaidh tú breac.
                                                  — Irish

When you're not fishing be mending the nets.

— Irish

The fed hound never hunts.   — English

Fish and visitors smell in three days.   — English

Don't think to hunt two hares with one hound.

— English

The fish will soon be caught that nibbles at
every bait.   — English

There is better fish in the sea than have ever
been caught.   — English

You cannot run with the hare and hunt with
the hounds.   — English

The best fishing is in the deepest waters.

— American

Fish or cut bait.   — American

All are not hunters that blow the horn.

— American

A rabbit is never caught twice in the same place.

— American

Ignorance

It takes a heap of licks to drive a nail in the dark.

— African American

Ignorance is the mother of superstition.

— English

Ignorance & Knowledge

God protect us from him who has read but
one book.
Dio mi guardi da quelli che hanno letto un
libro solo. — Italian

Knowledge has bitter roots but sweet fruits.
La radice del sapere é amara, ma tanto piú dolci
sono i suoi frutti. — Italian

Ignorance is a voluntary misfortune.
L'ignoranza é volontaria sciagura. — Italian

One who knows everything at times draws water
with a basket. — Igbo

One who explains things to an intelligent person
need not tire herself out talking. — Gandan

319

The brains don't lie in the beard.   — English

He that knows nothing, doubts nothing.
                                        — English

It is better to conceal one's knowledge than to
reveal one's ignorance.   — English

Where ignorance is bliss, 'tis folly to be wise.
                                        — English

Laugh and show your ignorance.   — American

It is better to know nothing than to half-know
many things.   — American

The less we know, the more we suspect.
                                        — American

Knowledge is proud that he knows so much; wisdom is humble that he knows no more.

— American

Indecision

She is as undecided as an orphan: if she does not wash her hands, she will be told that she is a dirty child; if she washes her hands she will be told that she is wasting water. — Malagasy

Do not have each foot on a different boat.

— Chinese

If you bow at all, bow low. — Chinese

Though you don't believe in other gods, you believe in the God of Thunder; though you don't believe in medicine generally, you believe in laxatives. — Chinese

Reticence builds a fortress in the mind.

— Chinese

Ingratitude

People count the refusals, [they] do not count
the gifts.   — Kikuyu

The gratitude that bees receive is the smoke that
people use to expel them and get at their honey.

— Swahili

The one who has helped others climb the ladder
gets kicked in the teeth.   — Swahili

In the midst of your illness you will promise a
goat, but when you have recovered a chicken will
seem sufficient.   — Junkun

Inspiration

A man's heart tells him of his opportunities better than seven watchmen on the lookout tower.
Lev enosh yagueed shi'eeyotav mishiva tzofeem al mitzpeh. — Hebrew

One person's candle furnishes light for many.
Ner l'echad, ner l'me'ah. — Hebrew

A quotation at the right moment is like bread to the hungry.
Pasuk bizmano k'nahama bish'at ra'ava. — Hebrew

Just as the world cannot exist without livelihoods, so it cannot exist without miracles and wonders.
Ma parnasa ee-efshar la'olam b'lo hee, kach ee-efshar la'olam b'lo niseem u'v'lo p'la'eem. — Hebrew

Judgement

If they are uttering insults and don't mean you, and yet you reply, you have condemned yourself.
— Tshi

It's because the rat knows what he does at night that he doesn't go out during the day.
— Haitian

Rare is the person who can weigh the faults of another without putting his thumb on the scale.
— Paraguayan

There can be no true pleasantry without discretion.
— Ecuadoran

Do not judge your neighbor until you walk two moons in his moccasins.   — Northern Cheyenne

Each person is his own judge.   — Piman

Take the drowning child from the water before
scolding it.   — Greboan

He hath good judgement that relieth not wholly
on his own.   — English

You can't judge a book by its cover.   — English

He who judges others condemns himself.
                                                 — American

We judge others by their acts, but ourselves by our
intentions.   — American

You are judged not by what you have but by what
you do with what you have.   — American

Justice

Justice is a good thing, only not in my house, but in my neighbor's.

*Justicia cosa muy buena, pero no en mi casa en
la ajena.*
— Cuban

The voice of the people is the will of God.
— Argentinean

One man's punishment is a deterrent to many.
Castigo de unos, escarmiento de muchos.
— Spanish

It's fair that he who tried to steal yours, loses his.
*Justo es que pierda lo suyo quien robar quiso
lo tuyo.*
— El Salvadoran

In a thousand pounds of law there is not one
ounce of love.
In cento libbre di legge, non v'é un'oncia di amore.
— Italian

We love the treason but hate the traitor.
Tradimento piace assai, traditor non piace mai.
— Italian

Equality of man is an empty phrase so long as it
does not exist among the world's peoples.
*Shivyon b'nai adam hee mila raika kol od ain
shivyon l'amai olam.* — Hebrew

Choose an easy death for one who must
be executed. — Hebrew

The voice of the people is like the voice of the Almighty.

Kol hamon, c'kol shadei. — Hebrew

The Torah can be interpreted in 49 different ways. God told Moses, "Decide according to the majority." — Hebrew

It's better that you suffer an injustice than you commit one.

Mutav she'teepaga me'ee tzedek me'asher ta'aseh avel l'zulatcha. — Hebrew

The world is sustained by three things: justice, truth, and peace.

Al shlosha d'vareem ha'olam kayam: al ha'deen, al ha'emet, v'al hashalom. — Hebrew

The whole arena tells them to kill the bull, yet the bull should kill no one.
Todos dicen que maten al toro, pero el toro no mate a nadie. — Mexican

He who gives what he can is no further obligated.
Quien da lo que puede no está obligado a más.
— Mexican

God speaks for the man who holds his peace.
Dios habla por el que calla. — Mexican

The crime accuses itself.
El delito acusa. — Mexican

Rain falls alike on the just and the unjust.
— Russian

He lived a colonel but died a corpse. — Russian

Messengers should be neither beheaded
nor hanged.   — Russian

Be just before you're generous.   — English

Justice delayed is justice denied.   — American

Without justice, courage is weak.   — American

Kindness

A big heart is better than a big brain.

— Swahili

Anticipate kindness from the happy person.

— Hausan

The only friendly cow is the one which gives milk.
— Kikuyu

If you see a man in a gown eating with a man in rags, the food belongs to the latter.   — Fulani

No matter how generous you are, you don't give your wife away.   — Tshi

Others will measure you with the same rod you use to measure them.
Con la vara que mides serás medido.   — Brazilian

No one has done good who has not suffered disillusionment.   — Chilean

You may light another's candle with your own without loss.   — Puerto Rican

When one is helping another, both gain in strength.   — Ecuadoran

The world rests on three things: the Bible,
religious worship, and deeds of loving kindness.
*Al pee shlosha d'vareem ha'olam omed: torah,
avodah, g'milut chasadeem.* — Hebrew

If two men claim your help, and one is your
enemy, help him first. — Hebrew

It's not the able that give, but the desirous.
No da el que puede, sino el que quiere.
— Mexican

Stupidity closes the doors of kindness.
La necedad cierra las puertas de la bondad.
— Mexican

The prickly pear has company only when it
bears fruit.
Al nopal lo van a ver sólo cuando tiene tunas.
— Mexican

Better to kiss a knave than be troubled with him.

       — English

Kindness is more binding than a loan.

       — American

A forced kindness deserves no thanks.

       — American

Speak kind words and you will hear kind answers.

       — American

Knowledge

Occasionally, a man with a right smart
education can't find his knife when it gets in
the wrong pocket.   — African American

To know all is to forgive all.   — American

When you persuade, speak of interest, not
of reason.   — American

Books speak to the mind, friends to the heart,
heaven to the soul, all else to the ears.
                                              — Chinese

A day of reading is a day of gain; a day without
reading is ten days of loss.   — Chinese

By filling one's head instead of one's pocket, one
cannot be robbed.   — Chinese

Who tells me of my faults is my teacher; who tells
me of my virtues does me harm.   — Chinese

The book and the sword descended from heaven together.
Hasefer v'hasayif yardu m'choracheem min hashameiyeem. — Hebrew

I learned much from my teachers, more from my friends, and the most from my pupils.
Harbeh lamad'tee merabotei u'mechaverei, umitalmeedei yoter mikuam. — Hebrew

Knowledge is like the sun—it dispels the darkness.
Hada'at cashemesh—v'hee tanees kol emesh. — Hebrew

Books provide knowledge, life furnishes understanding.
Mi'yad hasefer hayedi'ah nitna, meepee hachayeem hahavanah. — Hebrew

People hate what they do not understand.
B'nai adam soneem l'davar sh'ainam m'veeneem.

— Hebrew

He who is ignorant at home is ignorant abroad.

— Mexican

Eyes that don't see have less to lament.
Ojos que no ven, tienen menos que sentir.

— Mexican

There is only one good—knowledge; there is only one evil—ignorance.

— Russian

No man can be a good ruler unless he has first been ruled.

— Russian

What Johnny will not teach himself, Johnny will never know.

— Russian

Can do is easily carried aboot wi' ane.

— Scottish

Out o' Davy Lindsay into Wallace. — Scottish

Law

When force is imposed, the law is a joke.
Cuando la fuerza se impone, la ley es una broma.

— Colombian

Don't go to law with the devil in the court of hell.
Ná téirigh chun dlí leis an diabhal 's an chúirt in ifreann.

— Irish

If you go to court leave your soul at home.

— Irish

It is better to exist unknown to the law.
I ngan fhios don dlí is fearr bheith ann.   — Irish

Don't demand your rights until you have the power.
Ná héiligh do cheart go bhfeicir do neart.   — Irish

Law is costly; shake hands and be friends.
                                                 — Irish

Necessity knows no law.
Níl aon dlí ar an riachtanas.   — Irish

Neither break a law nor make one.
Ná bris reacht is ná déan reacht.   — Irish

Law cannot persuade where it cannot punish.
                                                 — English

Laws catch flies but lets hornets go free.

— English

Law governs man, and reason the law.

— English

A man who is his own lawyer has a fool for
a client.   — English

There's one law for the rich and another for
the poor.   — English

Better no law than a law not enforced.

— American

He knows not the law who knows not the
reason thereof.   — American

Where law ends, tyranny begins.　　— American

Laws too gentle are seldom obeyed; too severe,
seldom executed.　　　　　　　　　　— American

Leadership

It is a fine thing to command, though it be only a
herd of cattle.　　　　— Dominican Republic

Gold, when beaten, shines.　　　　— Peruvian

The emperor is the father of his people, not a
master to be served by slaves.　　　— Chinese

One who is fit to sit facing the south.
　　　　　　　　　　　　　　　— Chinese

Pull a strand of silk from a tangled mass.

— Chinese

Killing a bad monarch is not to be considered
murder but justice. — Chinese

By learning to obey, you will know how
to command.
Imparando a ubbidire s'impara a comandare.

— Italian

A leader is not necessarily one who knows the way
but one who thinks he knows the way.
*L'manheeg na'aseh al pee rov lo mee sheyodai'a et
haderech.* — Hebrew

We must not appoint a leader over the
community without first consulting the people.

— Hebrew

The rabbi is just the man who knows the Torah—
he is not the Torah itself.
*Harav aino elah yodai torah—aval aino
hatorah atzma.* — Hebrew

A good chief gives, he does not take.
— Mohawk

Great chiefs prove their worthiness. — Senecan

He who would rule must hear and be deaf, see
and be blind. — English

An illiterate king is a crowned ass. — English

If the blind lead the blind, both shall fall into
the ditch. — English

Learning

What de good a education if him got
no sense?   — Jamaican

Wealth, if you use it, comes to an end; learning, if
you use it, increases.   — Swahili

To come out of one's house means learning.
                                             — Kikuyu

A hunter has no mysterious notions about
the forest.   — Shonan

Learn weeping and thou shalt gain laughing.
                                             — English

If the brain sows not corn, it plants thistles.
                                             — English

Learning makes a good man better and a bad
man worse.   — English

Wise men learn from other men's mistakes; fools
insist on learning from their own.   — American

Learn as you'd live forever; live as you'd
die tomorrow.   — American

Life

Life can be understood backwards, but we live
it forwards.   — Swahili

Arriving and leaving, hoping and remembering,
that's what life consists of.   — Haitian

Living life is not like just crossing a field.
                                        — Russian

There were people before us and there will be
people after us.   — Russian

Worship the gods of where you live.   — Russian

Plan your life as though you were going to live
forever, but live today as if you were going to
die tomorrow.   — Russian

Life and misery began together.   — English

When the blind leads the way, woe to those
who follow.
Cuando los ciegos guían, ay de los que van detrás.
                                              — Honduran

A live dog is better than a dead lion.   — English

He that lives in hope dances to an ill tune.

— English

He who lives by the sword dies by the sword.

— English

Life liveth not in living, but in liking.   — English

A long life may not be good enough, but a good life is long enough.   — American

A life of leisure and a life of laziness are different things.   — American

Life is a comedy to those who think, a tragedy to those who feel.   — American

Life Lessons (Wisdom)

Better to beg forgiveness than to ask permission.
Más vale pedir perdón, que pedir permiso.

— Colombian

One never falls but on the side toward which
one leans. — Ecuadoran

Science makes men arrogant; wealth makes them
fools.
La ciencia hace soberbios; la fortuna necios.

— Bolivian

Don't take every ill to the doctor, or every quarrel
to the lawyer, or every thirst to the tavern.

— Uruguayan

Every time you forgive a man you weaken him
and strengthen yourself. — American

Never complain. Never explain.　　　— American

A nickel will get you on the subway, but garlic will get you a seat.　　　— American

Livelihood

Earning a living is as hard as splitting the Red Sea.
Kasha parnasa k'kri'at yam suf.　　　— Hebrew

Which is a man's most desirable occupation? The one for which he is most fit.
Aizohee ha'avoda ha'r'tzu'a l'adam b'yoter? Zo shela hu mat'eem b'yoter.　　　— Hebrew

The needle, small and thin, can support a man and his family.
Hamachat, katan v'dak, viyichalkel guever uvaito.
　　　— Hebrew

He that is at ease seeks dainties.   — English

Love

To stay together is to know each other.
                                                — Kikuyu

[*The*] one who loves an unsightly person is the
one who makes him beautiful.   — Gandan

He who loves, loves you with your dirt.
                                                — Ugandan

Where distrust enters, love is no more than
a boy.   — Chilean

A love that can last forever takes but a second to
come about.   — Cuban

Absence is the enemy of love; as the distance is from the eyes, so it is from the heart.

— Dominican Republic

Love looks through spectacles that make copper look like gold, poverty like riches, and tears like pearls.

— Peruvian

May the sun set on where my love dwells.

— Bolivian

Two in harmony are in God's company.

— Argentinean

Love is deed and not fine phrases.

— Puerto Rican

Find as much love as was given by your father and mother many times.

— Uruguayan

Love flies away and the pain remains.

— Bolivian

He who loves you will make you weep.

— Argentinean

To love and be wise is impossible.

— Colombian

Love me, love my dog.

— Chinese

Love and prudence are absolutely incompatible.

— Bolivian

Love and attention make all things grow.

— Chinese

Love itself is calm; turbulence arrives from
individuals.

— Chinese

Love for a person must extend to the crows on
his roof.   — Chinese

Love rules his kingdom with a sword.
Amor regge il suo regno senza spada.   — Italian

The more physical the love, the more sublime.
L'amore quanto piú é bestia, tanto piú sublime.
                                             — Italian

We leave to death the immortality of glory, but we
leave to life the immortality of love.
*Lasciamo ai morti l'immortaliá della gloria, ma
diamo ai viv l'immortaliá dell'amore.*   — Tagorean

Love is the ultimate deception of our life.
Amor di nostra vita ultimo inganno.   — Italian

Love, should I escape your snares, I doubt that I can be trapped by any other means.

Amor, s'io posso uscir de' tuci artigi, appeno reder posso che alcuno altro uncin mai piu mi pigli.

— Italian

The extreme form of passionate love is secret love.

Koi no shigoku wa shinobugoi. — Japanese

To the partial eyes of a lover, pockmarks seem like dimples.

Horeta yoku-me ni ya abata mo ekubo.

— Japanese

Love lives in palaces as well as in thatched cottages.

Ai wa kyuden no mo waraya ni mo sumu.

— Japanese

Love and a cough cannot be hidden.
Koi to seki to wa kakusarenu. — Japanese

Each has his Yang Chi.
Mei-mei no Yoki-hi. — Japanese

I'll give away rice fields and footpaths.
Ta mo yaro aze mo yaro. — Japanese

Better blind of eye than blind of heart.
Tov ivair aineiyeem mai'ivair lev. — Hebrew

Three things have a flavor of the world to come:
Sabbath, the sun, and married love.
*Shlosha me'en olam haba: Shabbat, shemesh,
v'tashmeesh.* — Hebrew

Love forgets dignity. — Hebrew

Love blinds the eyes to faults, and hatred blinds
the eyes to virtues.
*Ha'ahava m'averet et ha'ainayeem mer'ot chesronot
v'hasina m'averet ha'ainayeem mer'ot yitronot.*
— Hebrew

Man was born for love. If he hates, he was born
in vain.
*Adam l'ahava nivra, v'eem sonai hu, l'cheenam
hu chei.*
— Hebrew

Love one another and do not strive for another's
undoing.
— Seneca

When you have learned about love, you have
learned about God.
— Fox

Love makes the owl seem prettier than a
white falcon.
— Russian

Best to be off wi' the auld love before we be on
wi' the new. — Scottish

Nipping and scarting's Scotch folk's wooing.
— Scottish

Kissing is cried down since the shaking o' hands.
— Scottish

Hunger's gude kitchen to a cauld potato, but a
wet divot to the lowe o' love. — Scottish

The measure of our sacrifice is the measure of
our love. — English

Whom we love best to them we say least.
— English

If you want to be loved, be loveable. — English

A man has a choice to begin love, but not to
end it.   — English

Cold pudding settles love.   — English

Love laughs at locksmiths.   — English

'Tis better to have loved and lost than never to
have loved at all.   — English

Choose your love, then love your choice.
                                           — American

He that falls in love with himself will have
no rivals.   — American

Love enters man through his eyes, woman
through her ears.   — American

Loyalty

The antelope detests the one who announces its whereabouts more than the one who sees it.

— Kikuyu

A servant serves a king, he serves the king well; a servant serves two kings, he is true to one.

— Igbo

Luck

Look to your enemy for a chance to succeed.

— Chinese

Fortune has a fickle heart and a short memory.

— Chinese

Better to be the beak of a chicken than the rump of an ox.

— Chinese

What first appears as a calamity may later bring
good fortune.   — Chinese

If there are no clouds there will be no rain.
                                           — Chinese

Failure is the mother of success.   — Chinese

An unlucky man falls on straw, but splits his nose
from a hidden stone.
Nofel al hateven v'noguef chotmo b'even.
                                           — Hebrew

Good care takes the head off bad luck.
Baineann an coimhead maith an ceann den tubaiste.
                                           — Irish

Sweep the house with a broom in May and you'll
sweep the luck of the house away.   — English

Ill luck is good for something.   — English

He that hath no ill fortune is troubled with good.
   — English

The devil's children have the devil's luck.
   — English

Luck is the idol of the idle.   — English

See a pin and pick it up, all the day you'll have good luck.   — English

If luck is with you, even your ox will give birth to a calf.   — American

Lucky men need no counsel.   — American

The only sure thing about luck is that it's sure
to change.   — American

Marriage

The one who is looking for a wife doesn't speak
contemptuously of women.   — Tshi

Getting married with a woman is nothing;
it's assuming the responsibility of marriage
that counts.   — Haitian

The way you got married is not the way you'll
get divorced.   — Haitian

Before you married keep you' two eye open; after
you married, shut one.   — Jamaican

It is a lonesome washing without a man's shirt
in it.
Is uaigneach an níochán nach mbíonn léine ann.

— Irish

Your son is your son until he marries but your
daughter is your daughter until you die.
*Is é do mhac do mhac go bpósann s'ach is í d'iníon
go bhfaighidh tú bás.* — Irish

Love is blind to blemishes and faults.
Ceilann searc ainimh is locht. — Irish

I would rather have a clever woman than a
rich one.
*B'fhearr liom bean na bhfiche seift ná bean na
bhfiche punt.* — Irish

Three things you cannot comprehend: the mind of a woman, the working of the bees, and the ebb and flow of the tide.
Na trí nithe is deacra a thuiscint: intleacht na mban, obair na mbeach, tuile is trá na mara.

— Irish

There is never an old brogue but there is a foot to fit it.
Níl aon tseanstoca ná faigheann seanbhróg.

— Irish

The only cure for love is marriage.
Níl aon leigheas ar an ngrá ach pósadh. — Irish

Marry a mountain woman and you will marry the mountain.
Pós bean tsléibhe is pósfaidh tú an sliabh uilig.

— Irish

There is no feast till a roast and no torment till a marriage.

Ní céasta go pósta is ní féasta go róstadh. — Irish

Marry in haste, repent at leisure.

Chi si sposa in fretta, stenta adagio. — Italian

Better to have a husband without love than with jealousy.

Meglio il marito senz'amore, che con gelosia.

— Italian

Even in heaven, it is not good to be alone.

Affeelu in gan aiden, siz nit gut tzu zein alain.

— Yiddish

A Jew without a wife will not find peace in this life.

Kol yehudee she'ain lo eesha sharu'ee b'lo shalom.

— Hebrew

Partnership is good only with your wife—and there are those who say this too is not certain.

Shitfis iz guit nor mit dein froi, un aintzegueh zog'n az dos iz oich nit zeecher. — Hebrew

If a man and his wife are deserving, God's presence is with them; if they are not deserving, fire consumes them.

Esh v'eesha zachu—hashchina bainaihem. Lo zachu, esh ochlatam. — Hebrew

When the wife is away, the husband is master of the house.

Haba'al sorer b'vaito eem ha'eesha aina babayit. — Hebrew

Marrying off a daughter is like loading cargo on a ship.

Bat l'hasa'ah—oneeya l'hatana. — Hebrew

Better alone unattached than unsuitably matched.
Es mejor estar solo que mal acompañado.

— Mexican

He who does not honor his wife dishonors
himself.   — Mexican

Works, and not words, are the proofs of love.

— Mexican

See how the boy is with his sister and you can
know how the man will be with your daughter.

— Plains Sioux

It's not good for anyone to be alone.

— Cheyenne

The night's too short to warrant marrying poor.

— Russian

The first snow does not mean winter, nor the first love marriage. — Russian

A young man should not marry yet, an old man not at all. — Russian

A' are gude lasses, but where do the ill wives come frae? — Scottish

He that has lost a wife and sixpence has lost sixpence. — Scottish

Fleas and a grining wife are waukrife bedfellows. — Scottish

Choose your wife on Saturday, not on Sunday. — Scottish

A man canna wive and thrive in the same year.

— Scottish

A kiss and a drink o' water mak but a wersh breakfast.

— Scottish

A dish o' married love right sune grows cauld, and dosens down to nane as folk grow auld.

— Scottish

One year of joy, another of comfort, and all the rest of content.

— English

He that marries late marries ill.

— English

Marry in Lent, and you'll live to repent.

— English

Put not thy hand between the bark and the tree.
                                    — English

The hardest step is over the threshold.
                                    — English

Marrying for love is risky, but God smiles on it.
                                    — American

Keep your eyes wide open before marriage; half-shut afterwards.   — American

Matchmaker

Whoever cannot lie cannot be a matchmaker.
Mee she'aino m'shaker aino yachol lihiyot shadchan.
                                    — Hebrew

A dog can't be a butcher, and a bachelor can't be a matchmaker.

Kelev aino yahol lihiyot katzav, v'ravak aino yachol lihiyot shadchan. — Hebrew

Matches may be made in heaven, but they are sold down here. — American

Maturity

You can't eat the rice cake in a picture.

E ni kaita mochi wa kuenu. — Japanese

It's no good trying to bite your navel.

Heso o kamedomo oyobanu. — Japanese

By seeing one spot you know the entire leopard.

Ippan wo mite zempyo wo shiru. — Japanese

A sutra in a horse's ear.
Uma no mimi ni nembutsu. — Japanese

Years know more than books. — English

Give her bells and let her fly. — English

Old sheep shouldn't dress in lambs' fashion.
— English

Save something for the man that rides the white
horse. — English

Memories

The person who excreted it may forget it, but the
one who steps in it does not. — Luyian

To trouble me is better than to forget me.
— Nupe

371

A man cannot undo his past. Can zebras wipe
away their stripes? — Namibian

Cooked rice grains sticking to the soles of the feet.
Ashi no ura ni meshitsubu. — Japanese

The spirit of a three-year-old lasts a hundred
years.
Mitsugo no tamashii hyaku made. — Japanese

Sparrows, though they live to be a hundred, do
not forget their dance.
Suzume hyaku made odori wo wasurezu.

— Japanese

The last benefit is most remembered.

— English

All complain for want of memory, but none for want of judgement.   — English

Injuries we write in marble, kindnesses in dust.
                                        — English

We have all forgot more than we remember.
                                        — English

Men

It is because of man [*that*] we wear swords.
                                        — Tshi

The rabbit has a saying which goes: "If you were born a male then you are given impossible tasks."
                                        — Tshi

The tears of a man drop onto his chest.
                                        — Ndebele

373

You cannot distinguish between a drunken man and a mad man until they have slept.

— Cuban

No man is content. — English

A man is as old as he feels, a woman as old as she looks. — English

Whatever man has done, man may do.

— English

Whatever Nature does least, man does most.

— American

The Mill

The mill cannot grind with the water that is past.
Ní fhéadann na muilte meilt leis an uisce a chuaidh thart. — Irish

It is hard for an empty bag to stand itself alone.
Is deacair dho mhála folamh seasamh díreach.
— Irish

If you don't want flour, do not go into the mill.
Murar maith leat do mhéar a ghearradh, ná cuir
roimh an chorrán é. — Irish

An oven and mill are nurseries of news.
— English

Moderation

If one eats less, one will taste more. — Chinese

To extend your life by a year, take one less bite
each meal. — Chinese

A bird cannot roost but on one branch. A mouse can drink no more than its fill from a river.

— Chinese

Economize now or suffer want later.   — Chinese

What ripens quickly, rots quickly.   — Gandan

Too far east is west.   — English

He who takes on too much squeezes little.
El que mucho abarca poco aprieta.

— El Salvadoran

He who eats until he is ill must fast until he is well.   — English

Is there no mean but fast or feast?   — English

A little wind kindles, much puts out the fire.

— English

Morality

The heart of a little child is like the heart
of Buddha.   — Chinese

The pure, upon seeing it pure, call it pure.

— Chinese

It is a little thing to starve to death; it is a serious
matter to lose one's virtue.   — Chinese

Sending charcoal in the snow is better than
adding flowers to a brocade.   — Chinese

Virtue bears its own fruits.
Mida tova osa perot.

— Hebrew

A dog's nose and a maid's knee are always cold.
— English

God looks to clean hands, not to full ones.
— English

Black will take no other hue. — English

Virtue which parleys is near surrender.
— English

He that walketh with the virtuous is one of them.
— English

Motivation

Even the best horse needs to be spurred.
El mejor caballo necesita espuelas. — Mexican

The loftier and more distant the ideal, the greater
its power to lift up the soul.

Ma sheha ideal yoter gavoha v'yoter rachok, ken
yigdal kocho l'romem et hanefesh. — Hebrew

A fish follows the bait. — English

Nature

A log may lie in the water for ten years, but it will
never become a crocodile. — Songhain

No matter how thoroughly a crow may wash, it
remains ever black. — Shona

You may be clever but you can never lose
your shadow. — Igbo

Cutting the ears of a mule will not make him
a horse. — African

Little by little, the bird builds her nest.
In bheagán is ina bheagán, mar thug an cat an meascán. — Irish

A swan would die with pride only for its black feet. — Irish

Every little frog is great in his own bog. — Irish

Of small account is a fly till it gets into the eye.
Is beag le rá an chuileog nó go dté sí ins an tsúil. — Irish

Moonlight and boiled rice.
Tsukiyo ni kome no meshi. — Japanese

Destroy a country, but its mountains and
rivers remain.
Kuni horobite sanga ari.   — Japanese

It [*river*] belongs neither to the sea nor to the
mountain.
*Umi [kawa] no mono tomo yama no mono tomo
tsukanu.*   — Japanese

As though a bird had flown up from under
your feet.
Ashimoto kara tori ga tatsu yo.   — Japanese

I would like to break off the flower, but the
branch is too high.
Hana wa oritashi, kozue wa takashi.   — Japanese

At a distance enjoy the fragrance of flowers.
Toki wa hana no ka.   — Japanese

To touch the earth is to have harmony with nature.
— Oglala Sioux

When man moves away from nature his heart
becomes hard.   — Lakota

Take only what you need and leave the land as
you found it.   — Arapaho

Every animal knows far more than you do.
— Nez Perce

Nature shines through the cat's eyes.
Briseann an duchas tri shuile an chait.   — Irish

The fall of a leaf is a whisper to the living.
— English

He who lives according to nature will never be poor, and he who lives according to opinion will never be rich. — English

He that plants trees loves others besides himself.
— English

Nature abhors a vacuum. — English

Neighbors

Anyone can buy a good house, but good neighbors are priceless. — Chinese

If at home you receive no visitors, then abroad you will have no host. — Chinese

If two neighbors want to fight, they will find a quarrel in a straw.
Char fhadaigh dis tine gan troid. — Irish

Mind what you must live by.   — English

Love your neighbor, yet pull not down your
hedge.   — English

A good lawyer makes a bad neighbor.

      — English

Obstinacy

When a centipede dies on the wall it does not
fall down.   — Chinese

Winning an argument does not mean one has
convinced one's opponent.   — Chinese

Opportunity

In the daytime do we chase the black goat.

      — Igbo

Crisis brings opportunity and change.

— Chinese

A dry finger cannot pick up salt.   — Chinese

Unless there is opposing wind, a kite cannot rise.

— Chinese

Life can never give security, it can only promise
opportunity.   — Chinese

Kisses are keys.   — English

Opportunity makes a thief.   — English

Milk the cow that standeth still.   — English

Keep yourself from the opportunity and God will
keep you from the sin.   — American

Weak men wait for opportunities, strong men make them. — American

Opportunities, like eggs, come one at a time. — American

The opportunity of a lifetime is seldom so labeled. — American

Optimism

For the bad weather, a cheerful face.
Al mal tiempo buena cara. — Nicaraguan

There's no ill that doesn't turn out for the better.
No hay mal que por bien no venga.
— Guatemalan

Daylight sho t'rough lilly keyhole.
— Jamaican

When God chooses to give, it shall come in through the door.
Al que Dios le ha de dar, por la puerta debe entrar.
— Haitian

Cheerfulness is the very flower of health.
Kaikatsu wa kenko ni saku hana da. — Japanese

One cannot always find a fish under a willow.
Yanagi no shita ni itsu-mo dojo wa inai.
— Japanese

It is one life, whether we spend it in laughing or in weeping.
Waratte kurasu mo issho, naite kurasu mo issho.
— Japanese

A fruit-bearing tree is known by its flowers.
Mi no naru ki wa hana kara shireru. — Japanese

Although the sun shines, leave not your cloak
at home.

*Non bisogna uscir senza mantello, per quanto il sole
risplende bello.* — Italian

Hope dies last of all.

La esperanza muere al último. — Mexican

Where one door closes, another one opens.

Cuando una puerta se cierra, otra se abre.

— Mexican

Half an orange tastes as sweet as a whole one.

— American

All things were once impossible. — American

Passions

It is better for the eyes to die than the heart.

— Swahili

What can be expected to be dropped is held in the hands, but what is in the heart I shall die with.

— Shona

To know another is not to know that person's face, but to know that person's heart.   — Chinese

The heart has reasons that reason does not understand.
Il cuore ha le sue ragioni e non intende ragione.

— Italian

The end of passion is the beginning of repentance.
La fine della passione é il principio del pentimento.

— Italian

Where passion is high, reason is low.
Quando é alta la passione, é bassa la ragione.

— Italian

When passion entereth at the foregate, wisdom
goeth out of the postern. — English

Master your passions or your passions will
master you. — English

A candle lights others and consumes itself.

— English

The belly teaches all arts. — English

One nail drives out another. — English

A man in passion rides a mad horse.

— American

He that shows a passion tells his enemy where he
may hit him.   — American

Absence cools moderate passions but inflames
violent ones.   — American

The passions are like fire and water: good servants
but bad masters.   — American

If passion drives, let reason hold the reins.
                                          — American

Pathways & Footpaths

"I see," said the blind man when he was directed
on his way.   — Irish

Half a leap falls into the ditch.
*An té ná fuil léim aige cuimlíodh sé a thóin
den gclaí.*   — Irish

A stirring foot always gets something, even if it's only a thorn. — Irish

The shortcut to food but the long way to work.
An congar chun an bhidh is an timpeall chun na hoibre. — Irish

A thorn, a hound's tooth, a fool's word: these are the three sharpest things.
Fiacal con, dealg láibe, nó focal amadáin: ná trí nithe is géire amuigh. — Irish

One look ahead is better than two looks behind.
Is fearr súil romhat ná dhá shúil id dhiaidh. — Irish

Darkness shows no wrong path to she who gets what she wants before dark. — Kikuyu

Pains and patience would take a snail to America.
Aimsir agus foighid, bhéarfadh sé an seilide go hIarúsailéim. — Irish

The fool wanders, the wise man travels.
— English

However far a man goes, he must start from his own door. — English

A trodden path bears no grass. — English

On an unknown path every foot is slow.
— American

The road to ruin is kept in good repair, and the travellers pay the expense. — American

Patience

A tree that has grown bent for thirty years cannot be straightened in one year.　　　— Tshi

However long the night, the dawn will break.
　　　　　　　　　　— Hausan

If patience hides something, anger won't search and get.　　　　　　— Mamprussi

If you find the river flooded, wait.　　— Swahili

"Hurry" and "well" never go hand in hand.
　　　　　　　　　　— Hatian

True patience consists in bearing what is unbearable.
Naranu kannin suru ga kannin.　　— Japanese

Sleep and wait for good luck.
Kaho wa nete mate. — Japanese

A short temper is a disadvantage.
Tanki wa sonki. — Japanese

A Buddha's face when asked three times.
Hotoke no kao mo san-do. — Japanese

If there is a lid that does not fit, there is a lid that does.
Awanu futa mo areba au futa mo ari.
— Japanese

Even dust amassed will grow into a mountain.
Chiri mo tsumoreba yama to naru. — Japanese

Paper is patient—you can put anything on it.
— Russian

Be patient, Cossack, and you'll be a chieftain.

— Russian

Praise a fair day at night. — Russian

Patience conquers destiny.
Buann an fhoighne ar an chinniuint. — Irish

When all is wet to the skin, hold out yet.

— English

Crumb not your bread before you taste your
porridge. — English

Patience is a bitter plant, but it has sweet fruit.

— English

He that can have patience can have what he will.

— American

Patience wears out stones.   — American

Peace/Good Wishes

If I am virtuous and worthy, for whom should I
not maintain a proper concern?   — Chinese

Laws are useless when men are pure,
unenforceable when men are corrupt.
                                         — Chinese

May it always be spring with you.   — Chinese

Where there is peace, God is.   — English

If you want peace, prepare for war.
                                         — English

Peace makes plenty.   — English

It is better to keep peace than to make peace.

— American

Perseverance

It is not enough for a man to know how to ride, he must also know how to fall.   — Puerto Rican

When the road is long, even slippers feel tight.
Cuando el camino es largo, hasta las zapatillas aprietan.   — Peruvian

There's no evil that lasts a hundred years, nor a body that can endure it.
No hay mal que dure cien años, ni cuerpo que lo resista.   — Cuban

The bird that pecks at a rock trusts in the strength of its beak.   — Ugandan

Sickness tells us what we are.
Le malattie ci dicono quel che siamo. — Italian

Patience is a flower that grows not in everyone's
garden.
*La pazienza é una buon'erba, ma non nasce in tutti
gli orti.* — Italian

Time and patience change the mulberry leaf
to satin.
Con la pazienza la foglia di gelso diventa seta.
— Italian

To be simple is a pedestrian virtue, but to per-
severe in simplicity is a virtue of spiritual giants.
*Lihiyot tameem, zo ma'ala bainoneet; ulam,
l'hatmeed bitmeenut, zo mima'alotaihem shel g'dolai
hanu'ach.* — Hebrew

Whom God favors, He tries with affliction.
*Kol she'hakadosh barush hu chafetz bo, m'dakk'o
b'yisurim.*   — Hebrew

Man is like a bird: a bird can fly higher and
higher, but only if its wings continue to move
without stopping.
*Ha'adam nimshal latzipor: b'chocha shel tzipor
la'alot mala, mala, bitnei shetanee'a et k'nafeha
blee heref.*   — Hebrew

Even when a sharp sword rests on your neck, don't
give up on mercy.
*Afeelu cherev chada munachat al tzavero shel adam,
al yimna atzmo min harachameem.*
                                               — Hebrew

The world's like a ladder: one ascends, and
one descends.
Ha'olam domeh l'sulam: zeh oleh v'zeh yored.
—Hebrew

Between the beginning and the end there is always
a middle. — Mexican

The first blin [pancake] always turns out lumpy.
— Russian

Better a stride that will last than a trot that
tires fast.
Más vale paso que dure y no trote que canse.
— Mexican

With patience and a bit of spittle, the elephant picks up the ant so little.
Con paciencia y salivita un elefante se coge a una hormiguita. — Mexican

The more you ask how far you have to go, the longer your journey seems. — Seneca

The pathway to glory is rough and many gloomy hours obscure it. — Chief Black Hawk

The longest road has an end and the straightest road has an end. — Irish

Prayer knocks till the door opens. — English

He who has carried the calf will be able by and by to carry the ox. — English

Where your will is ready your feet are light.

— English

Persevance is failing nineteen times and
succeeding the twentieth. — American

Perspective

One-eye man a king a blind country.

— Jamaican

A one-eyed person does not thank God until he
meets a blind person at prayer. — Nigerian

The person to whom things are brought does not
know the length of the road. — Ovambo

The worm don't see nothing pretty in the
robin's song. — African American

He who doesn't look ahead gets left behind.
El que adelante no ve, atrás se queda.
— Venezuelan

Do not fear a stain that disappears with water.
— Puerto Rican

A frog in the well knows not the ocean.
Ido no kawazu taikai wo shirazu. — Japanese

He who never goes is a fool; he who goes twice is also a fool.
Ichido yukanu baka, nido yuku baka. — Japanese

One sees the sky through a hollow reed.
Yoshi no zui kara tenjo o miru. — Japanese

There are seventy ways of interpreting the Bible.
Shiveem paneem latorah. — Hebrew

Just as people's faces are different, so are their opinions different.

K'shem she'ain partzufai b'nai adam domeem, kach ain dai'otaihem domot. — Hebrew

Night was created so that we might consider what we did during the day.

Haleilah nivra lachashov bo ma'aseh hayom.
— Hebrew

When you're in a strange city, adopt its manners.

Azalta l'karta halech b'nimusa. — Hebrew

When young, it's all dreams; when old, all memories.

Cuando joven, de ilusiones; cuando viejo, de recuerdos. — Mexican

Time heals and then it kills.
El tiempo cura y nos mata. — Mexican

Though the cage be made of gold, it's still
a prison.
Aunque la jaula sea de oro, no deja de ser prisión.
— Mexican

Blue are the hills that are far away. — Scottish

I'm speaking o' hay and you o' horse corn.
— Scottish

In every beginning, think of the end. — English

You must look where it is not as well as where
it is. — English

Philosophy

A rosy face in the morning, white bones in
the evening.
Ashita no kogan, yube no hakkotsu. — Japanese

Life is a candle before the wind.
Jinsei wa fuzen no tomoshibi. — Japanese

To leap into a pool embracing a stone.
Ishi wo idaite fuchi ni iru. — Japanese

A willow before the wind.
Yanagi ni kaze. — Japanese

To one who does not wander there is not
enlightenment.
Mayowanu mono ni satori nashi. — Japanese

The splendor of the rose of Sharon is but a day.
Kinka ichi-jitsu no ei. — Japanese

It is not the beard that makes the philosopher.
— English

Philosophy means being able to explain why you are happy when you are poor. — American

Pragmatism

It is better to go home and make your net than to gaze longingly at the fish in the deep pool.
Fuchi ni nozomite uo wo urayamu wa shirizoite ami wo musubi ni shikazu. — Japanese

Even a superb hawk will not catch game unless it is loosed.
Ichimotsu no taka mo hanatazareba torazu.

— Japanese

One cannot become a priest just by having
a rosary.
Juzu bakari de osho wa dekinu. — Japanese

Crabs dig holes according to the size of
their shells.
Kani wa kora ni nisete ana o horu. — Japanese

For rice cakes, go to the rice-cake maker.
Mochi wa mochiya. — Japanese

If you would shoot a general, shoot first his horse.
Sho wo in to seba mazu uma wo iyo. — Japanese

Fire does not burn in a jar.
Tsubo no naka de wa hi wo moenu. — Japanese

Cap no fit you, you no tek i' up. — Jamaican

Bad water also quenches the fire.

— Mamprussi

The river is crossed where it is shallow.

— Kikuyu

Make not the door wider than the house.

— English

Pride

Rooster makes mo' racket dan de hen w'at lay
de aig.   — African American

Boastin' man brudder a de liar.   — Jamaican

Gluttony and vanity grow with age.
Gula y vanidad crecen con la edad.   — Cuban

Time will give you the best disguise.
El mejor disfraz el tiempo te lo dará.

— Uruguayan

Abundance breeds arrogance.
La abundancia da arrogancia.   — Argentinean

You praise yourself so much you're never finished.
Tanto te alabas que nunca acabas. — Argentinean

Never be boastful; someone may come along who
knew you as a child.   — Chinese

Pride breakfasted with plenty, dined with poverty,
and supped with infamy.
*L'orgoglio fa colazione con l'abbondanza, pranza con
la povertá e cena con la vergogna.*   — Italian

Vainglory blossoms but never bears.
La vanagloria é un fiore che mai non porta frutta.
— Italian

Pride costs us more than hunger, thirst, and cold.
— English

It is pride, not nature, that craves much.
— English

Pride in prosperity turns to misery in adversity.
— English

To be proud of knowledge is to be blind
with light.   — American

Pride that dines on vanity sups on contempt.
— American

Pride is the last vice a good man gets clear of.

— American

Proverbial Wisdom

Proverbs in conversation are torches in darkness.

— Venezuelan

A proverb is to speech what salt is to food.

— Panamanian

If you want to please, never say things are
going well.
*Si quieres quedar bien, nunca digas que te va
muy bien.* — Haitian

A rolling stone gathers no moss, but it gets a
great shine.
Cha chruinnionn cloch chasaidh caonach. — Irish

Proverbs

A person can understand things deeply
through proverbs.
*Al y'dai hamashaleem yored ha'adam l'omek
hadevareem.* — Hebrew

A pointed proverb is like a diamond: it emits
light, and it also cuts.
*Hamichtav hatov c'yahalom yivade'a, mefeetz noga
af pole'ach u'voke'a.* — Hebrew

No proverb is untrue.
Ain pitgam cozev. — Hebrew

Proverbs are the children of experience.
— English

Wise men make proverbs but fools repeat them.
— English

The wit of one man, the wisdom of many.

— English

Prudence

He who marries prudence is the brother-in-law
of peace. — Bolivian

If I listen I have the advantage, if I speak others
have it. — Peruvian

Speak whenever you must, hush whenever
you can.
Habla siempre que debas, y calla siempre que puedas.
— Panamanian

Say nothing about another that you wouldn't want
to hear about yourself.
De ninguno has de decir lo que de ti no quieres oír.
— El Salvadoran

The wise man affirms little and doubts much.
De sabios es poco afirmar y mucho dudar.

— Panamanian

He who speaks much, errs much.
El que mucho habla, mucho yerra. — Cuban

Be frugal in prosperity, fear not in adversity.

— Chinese

Listen to all, pluck a feather from every passing
goose, but follow no one absolutely.

— Chinese

A fool's heart is found in his mouth.

— Chinese

Silence condemns more effectively than loud
accusations. — Chinese

Think before you speak but do no speak all that
you think.   — Chinese

He who eats globefish soup is a fool; so is he who
does not.
Fugu-jiru kuu baka, kuwanu baka.   — Japanese

The spit aimed at the sky comes back to one.
Ten ni mukatte tsuba o haku.   — Japanese

When the hand is put in, the foot follows.
Te ga ireba ashi mo iru.   — Japanese

Dumplings are better than flowers.
Hana yori dango.   — Japanese

Consult anyone, even your knees.
Hiza tomo dango.   — Japanese

The mouth is the cause of calamity.
Kuchi wa wazawai no moto.
— Japanese

Having conquered, tighten the thongs of your helmet.
Katte kabuto no o wo shimeyo.
— Japanese

A grain of prudence is worth a pound of craft.
— English

One half the troubles in this world can be traced to saying "yes" too quick or to saying "no" not soon enough.
— American

Realism

Even Confucius had his misfortunes.
Koshi mo toki ni awazu.
— Japanese

Ten men, ten tastes.
Ju-nin to-iro. — Japanese

Don't estimate the value of a badger skin before catching the badger.
Toranu tanuki no kawa-zan'yo. — Japanese

From gods that are left alone, there is no curse.
Sawaranu kami ni tatari nashi. — Japanese

In trying to straighten the horns you kill the ox.
Tsuno wo tamete ushi wo korosu. — Japanese

The cow drinks water and it turns to milk; the snake drinks water and it turns to poison.
Ushi wa mizu wo nonde chichi to shi, hebi wa mizu wo nonde doku to su. — Japanese

Dreams are what you hope for; reality is what you plan for.   — American

Reality never surpasses imagination.

— American

Regret

What is past and cannot be prevented should not be grieved for.   — Pawnee

Life is both giving and receiving.   — Mohawk

Careless hurry may cause endless regret.

— American

Fret today, regret tomorrow.   — American

Youth is a blunder, manhood a struggle, old age a regret.   — American

Religion

The nearer the church, the further from God.
An té is giorra dhon teampall, ní hé is giorra dhon altóir.
— Irish

All are not saints that go to church.
— Irish

Don't be too friendly with the clergy and don't fall out with them.
Ná bí róbheag is ná bí rómhór leis an gcléir.
— Irish

Put the priest in the middle of the parish.
— Irish

A Sabbath well-spent brings a week of content.
— Irish

It cannot be true religion if it loves money.
Ain dat eem ahavat betza.
— Hebrew

Science without religion is lame; religion without science is blind.

Hamada blee dat tzole'a; hadat blee mada iveret.

— Hebrew

More than the Jewish people preserved the Sabbath, the Sabbath preserved them.

Yoter mi'yisra'el shamra et hashabbast, shamra hashabbat otam.

— Hebrew

No man's religion ever survived his morals.

— English

He that after sinning mends, recommends himself to God.

— English

A man without religion is a horse without a bridle.

— English

Religion is the best armor in the world, but the worst cloak. — American

You're not supposed to keep religion, it's supposed to keep you. — American

Renting

An empty house is better than a bad tenant.
Is fearr teach folamh ná drochthionónta. — Irish

Cleaning the house will not pay the rent.
Ní teach glan a íocfas cíos. — Irish

The well-fed does not understand the lean.
Ní thuigeann an sách an seang. — Irish

Your lord's rent or your child's life.
Cíos do thiarna nó bia do linbh. — Irish

Reputation

All kind of fish eat man, only shark get blame.
— Jamaican

A man dies but his tongue [*his words*] does
not rot. — Twi

He who is wont to provoke others is called a
provoker even when he is provoked. — Kikuyu

A dog which steals leaves its puppies a bad name.
— Kaonde

There are three crowns: Bible, priesthood, royalty.
But the crown of a good name surpasses them all.
Shlosha k'tareem hem: Torah, k'huna, v'malchut.
Keter shem tov oleh al kulam. — Hebrew

There is nothing better than a good reputation.
— Hebrew

Honor is greater than wealth; wealth is only an instrument to attain honor.
Hakavod hu yoter m'uleh min ha'osher, she'ain ha'osher kee eem klee l'haguee el hakavod.
— Hebrew

The clown is best in his own country, and the gentleman anywhere.
— Mexican

Better to be red-faced once than 100 times purple.
Más vale una vez colorado que ciento descolorido.
— Mexican

The fathers ate the cranberries and the children are left with the aftertaste.
— Russian

Take care of your dress from when it's new and
your honor from your youth.　　　— Russian

Ae man may steal a horse where another daurna
look ower the hedge.　　　　　— Scottish

Where MacGregor sits is head of the table.
　　　　　　　　　　　　— Scottish

He that sleeps wi' dogs maun rise wi' fleas.
　　　　　　　　　　　　— Scottish

Reputation is commonly measured by the acre.
　　　　　　　　　　　　— English

A good reputation stands still; a bad one runs.
　　　　　　　　　　　　— American

It is not often that a man's reputation outlasts
his money.   — American

Respect

Take the bull by the horns and the man at
his word.
*Agarra al toro por los cuernos, al hombre por la
palabra.*   — Colombian

If you would be respected in company, seek the
society of your equals and not of your superiors.
                                             — Cuban

Treat the lesser as you would have the greater
treat you.   — Venezuelan

How can swallows and sparrows know the
thoughts of a great swan?
Enjaku nanzo koko no kokorozashi wo shiran ya?
                                             — Japanese

Borrowed garments do not fit well.
Karigi wa mi ni awanu.   — Japanese

Look at the man you serve and you will see how
much you are esteemed.   — Mexican

Respect for the rights of others is peace.
El respeto al derecho ajeno es la paz.   — Mexican

To be a public man is slavery.   — American

One who cannot respect himself cannot
respect another.   — American

Responsibility

No one roasts rotten meat and puts it in the
mouth of their friend and then says "Your
mouth stinks."   — Tshi

We must blame the thief first before we say that where the owner put her property [*was*] improper.
— Yoruban

To forget one's ancestors is to be a brook without a source, a tree without a root.   — Chinese

One guest does not trouble two hosts.
— Chinese

If every man would sweep before his own door, the city would soon be clean.
Se ognun spazzasse da casa sua, tutta la cittá sarebbe netta.   — Italian

If everyone cleaned his own doorstep, all the streets would be clean.
Lu nika eesh'eesh lifnai pitcho, v'nuku eretz v'chutzot.   — Hebrew

A person is always responsible: if his act was
accidental or intentional, whether he was awake
or asleep.
*Adam mu'ad l'olam: bain shog'eg, bain mezeed, bain
er, bain yashen.* — Hebrew

Look after me, and I'll look after you.
Shomr lee va'eshmor l'cha. — Hebrew

All Jews are responsible, one for another.
Kol yisrael araivin zeh bazeh. — Hebrew

He that blames would buy. — English

"What a dust we kick up," as the fly said to the
cart wheel.
*"Nach mise a thog an dusta?" arsa an chuileog i
ndiaidh and choiste.* — Irish

The more responsibilities a man assumes, the more likely he is to meet them.   — American

Righteousness

I was young, now I'm old, and I did not see a righteous man forsaken and his children begging for bread.

Na'ar hayeetee gam zakantee v'lo ra'eetee tzadeek ne'ezav v'zar'o m'vakesh lechem.   — Hebrew

There are three people whose lives are unworthy— the overly compassionate, the hot-tempered, and the hypercritical.   — Hebrew

In my life of vanity I saw everything: a righteous man dying in his righteousness, and a wicked man living long after his evil deeds.

Et hakol ra'eetee bi mai chevlee: yesh tzadeek oved b'tzidko v'yesh rasha ma'areech b'ra'ato.   — Hebrew

Risk

When a ship is broken, the accident does not
prevent others from sailing.　　　— Martinique

He who doesn't risk a penny doesn't make a peso.
El que no arriesga un real, no gana un peso.
　　　　　　　　　　　　　　　— Guatemalan

No risk, no gain.　　　　　　　　　— English

There's a risk in every jump.
Todo salto tiene riesgo.　　　　　— Puerto Rican

Scotland

A Scots mist will weet an Englishman to the skin.
　　　　　　　　　　　　　　　— Scottish

The Englishman greets, the Irishman sleeps, but
the Scotchman gangs till he gets it.　　— Scottish

Scotsmen aye tak their mark frae a mischief.
　　　　　　　　　　　　　　— Scottish

I hae a Scotch tongue in my head—if they speak
I'se answer.　　　　　　　　— Scottish

Carrick for a man, Kyle for a coo, Cunningham
for corn and ale, and Galloway for woo'.
　　　　　　　　　　　　　　— Scottish

Selfishness

The flowers of others are red.
Hito no hana wa akai.　　　　　— Japanese

To lend your hatchet and get your forest cut down.
Nata wo kashite yama wo kirareru.　　— Japanese

A miser and his persimmon seeds.
Shiwambo no kaki no tane. — Japanese

He draws water over his own rice field.
Onore no ta ni mizu wo hiku. — Japanese

Who eats his cock alone must saddle his
horse alone. — English

Sensitivity

Even a one-inch insect has a half-inch soul.
Issun no mushi ni mo go-bu no tamashii.
— Japanese

People with the same disease share sympathy.
Idobata no chawan. — Japanese

Shame

A tea cup on the edge of a well.
Dobyo ai-awaremu. — Japanese

Fallen blossoms do not return to branches; a
broken mirror does not again reflect.
Rakka eda ni kaerazu, hakyo futatabi terasazu.
— Japanese

To commit harakiri with a pestle.
Rengi de hara kiru. — Japanese

Whether it was the tenant who seduced the
landlord's wife, or the landlord who seduced the
tenant's wife, it is the tenant who would leave
the house. — Igbo

Tell the truth and shame the devil. — English

Past shame, past grace.   — English

You will find enough of brushna in every wood to burn it.
Ta a loscadh fein i ngach coill.   — Irish

Truth may be blamed but never shamed.
                                           — American

Sin

That which is a sin in others is a virtue in ourselves.   — Chilean

Break the leg of a bad habit.   — Puerto Rican

One washes the body in vain if one does not wash the soul.   — Cuban

For a new sin, a new penance.   — Venezuelan

He who overcomes his passions overcomes his greatest enemies. — Colombian

The beginning of sin is sweet; its end is bitter.
Raishai d'chetya chalai v'sofai mareer.
— Hebrew

From a limb that started sinning, all the troubles began.
Ever shehitcheel ba'avera, mimenu matchelet hapuranut. — Hebrew

It's not the sin that maddens a person but the desire to do it.
Lo ha'avera atzma ma'aveera et ha'adam al da'ato, ela hata'ava la'avera. — Hebrew

Flee from sin as from a snake; if you go near it, it will bite you.
K'mipnai nachash nus min chet, v'eem tikrav elecha yishcheka. — Hebrew

There are people who deserve paradise for their thoughts, and hell for their deeds.
Yesh r'u'yeem b'ad mach'sh'votaihem gan eden u'v'ad ma'asaihem l'gaihinom. — Hebrew

The gambler breaks all of the Ten Commandments.
Hakubi'yustus over al kol aseret hadibrot.
— Hebrew

Whoever has not tasted sinfulness does not qualify for holiness.
Mee shelo ta'am chet lo huchshar likdusha.
— Hebrew

Even a small thorn causes festering.
Is beag an dealg a dheanas sileadh. — Irish

Men are punished by their sins, not for them.
— American

Sin concealed needs two forgivings.
— American

He that swims in sin will sink in sorrow.
— American

Do not make me kiss and you will not make
me sin. — English

It is sin to steal a pin. — English

A sin confessed is half forgiven. — English

Old sins have long shadows.   — English

Sincerity

Behind the gentle barb lies the deadly barb.
Tras las burlas suaves vienen las burlas graves.
                                        — Haitian

Faces of men we see but not their hearts.
                                        — Cuban

When a man repeats a promise again and again,
he means to fail you.   — English

Examine well the counsel that favours your desire.
                                        — English

That which comes from the heart is always
sincere.   — American

Sorrow

Sorrow also sings, when it runs too deep to cry.
También de dolor se canta cuando llorar no se puede.
— Mexican

A bellyful is one of meat, drink, or sorrow.
— English

The saddest dog sometimes wags its tail.
— English

Sorrow is always dry.
— English

Sorrow remembered sweetens present joy.
— English

The safest antidote against sorrow is employment.
— English

Earth has no sorrow that heaven cannot heal.

— American

Sport

The morning of the race is not the morning to
feed your horse.

*Tá sé rómhall croisín a chur faoi theach nuair a
thiteas sé.* — Irish

The best horse doesn't always win the race.

Is minic nach é an capall is fearr a thóigeas an rása.
— Irish

Dancing was first started by a madman. — Irish

A good candle-holder proves a good gamester.

— English

Status

Although shrimps may dance around, they do not leave the river.   — English

A king's face should show grace.   — English

Eat not cherries with the great.   — English

Noble birth is a poor dish at table.   — English

The cat has leave to look at the queen and the queen has leave to shoot it.
Ta cead ag an gcat breathnu ar an mbanrion.
                  — Irish

The bean paste that smells like bean paste is not the best quality.
Miso no miso-kusai wa jo-miso ni arazu.
                  — Japanese

The clog and Amida [*Buddha*] are both from the same piece of wood.
Geta mo Amida [Hotoke] mo onaji ki no hashi.

— Japanese

Eggplants do not grow on melon vines.
Uri no tsuru ni nasubi wa naranu.   — Japanese

Strategy

A lame cat is better than a swift horse when rats infest the palace.   — Chinese

Beat the grass to frighten the snakes.   — Chinese

Three simple shoemakers equal one brilliant strategist.   — Chinese

If one man guards a narrow pass, ten thousand cannot get through.   — Chinese

Success

One who says "It was too much for me" does
not try.   — Gandan

The area covered by your life is not as important
as what you build on it.   — Swahili

A good surgeon must have a hawk's eye, a lion's
heart and a woman's hand.
                        — Dominican Republic

Among the weak, the strongest is the one who
doesn't forget his weakness.   — Panamanian

If you want no disappointments, don't indulge
in illusions.
Si no quieres decepción, no te hagas ilusión.
                                    — Panamanian

It takes true heroism to conquer oneself.

— Chinese

Without oars you cannot cross in a boat.
Rokai ga note fune de watarenu.   — Japanese

You cannot catch a tiger cub unless you enter the tiger's den.
Koketsu ni irazumba koji o ezu.   — Japanese

Too many accomplishments make no accomplishment.
Tagei wa mugei.   — Japanese

A dog that walks around will find a stick.
Inu mo arukeba bo ni ataru.   — Japanese

Fall down seven times, get up eight.
Nana-korobi ya-oki.   — Japanese

If a waterwheel exerts itself, it has no time to get frozen.

Sei daseba, koru ma mo nashi mizuguruma.

— Japanese

Even a thousand-mile journey begins with the first step.

Sen-ri no michi mo ippo kara. — Japanese

Even though you tread slowly over your rice field it will become muddy.

Sorosoro ittemo ta wa nigoru. — Japanese

Real success is success of the soul.

Hahatzlacha ha'ameeteet hee hatzlachat hanefesh.

— Hebrew

If I am not for myself, who will be?

Eem ain a'nee lee, mee lee? — Hebrew

If you don't aspire to great things, you won't attain small things.
Eem lo tish'af ligdolot, ad hak'tanot lo tavo.

— Hebrew

Sometimes the position does not make the man, but the man makes the position.
L'eeteem lo hamisra osa et ha'adam elah ha'adam oseh et hamisra.

— Hebrew

Whoever pursues fame and greatness, they flee from him; whoever shuns greatness, it comes after him.
Kol hamechazer al hag'dula, g'dula borachat mimenu; kol haborai'ach min hag'dula, hag'dula m'chazeret acharav.

— Hebrew

No one can bind himself to perform the impossible.

— Mexican

When it's time to fry the beans, you can't do without lard.

A la hora de freir frijoles, lo que hace falta es la manteca. — Mexican

Ten who shout obtain more than ten who remain silent. — Mexican

No man's a prophet in his own land.
Nadie is profeta en su tierra. — Mexican

A bold attempt is half of success. — English

You can't be a howling success by simply howling. — American

If we blame others for our failures, we should also give them credit for our success. — American

To be successful in love, one must know how to begin and when to stop. — American

Suitability

Dancing [*to*] the drum will be done where the drum is. — Igbo

Nebber mek you sail too big fe you ship. — Jamaican

A cart-horse could never win the Derby. — Irish

Superiority

What the superior man seeks in himself, the small man seeks in others. — Chinese

It takes a tree ten years to mature; it takes a man one hundred years to form. — Chinese

The mighty tree must catch the wind.

— Chinese

If you do a person a favor, you'll be his superior; if he does one for you, his inferior; and if neither, you'll be his friend.

Eem ta'aseh chesed la'adam tihiye g'veero; v'eem t'kabel chesed, tihiye aseero; v'eem lo titztarech, tihiye chavero. — Hebrew

He who can take advice is sometimes superior to those who give it. — American

Superstition

Speak to the devil and you'll hear the clatter of his hooves.

Trácht ar an diabhal agus taispeánfaidh sé é féin.

— Irish

Pulling the devil by the leg is a bad grip.
Ag tarraingt an diabhail de ghreim eireabaill.

— Irish

A good heart never went to hell.
Níor chuaigh fial riamh go hifreann. — Irish

It's hard to kill a bad thing.
Is doiligh drochrud a mharú. — Irish

A dimple in the chin, your living comes in; a
dimple in the cheek, your living to seek.

— English

Suspicion

One's village is revealed.
Osata ga shireru. — Japanese

Inquire seven times then doubt a person.
Nantabi tazunete hito wo utagae. — Japanese

Trash accumulates in stagnant water.
Yodomizu ni gomi tamaru. — Japanese

Snakes follow the way of serpents.
Ja no michi wa hebi. — Japanese

Caesar's wife must be above suspicion.

— English

Too much force breeds suspicion. — American

Taste

If there was not bad taste, goods would not
be sold. — Panamanian

Taste in variety, variety in taste. — Nicaraguan

453

No accounting for taste.   — English

'Tis the taste that tells the tale.   — American

Temptation

When the treasure chest is open, even the just man sins.
En arca abierta, hasta el justo peca.   — Ecuadoran

He who steals in order to give to God can only get advice from the devil.   — Nicaraguan

He who avoids the temptations avoids the sin.
      — Guatemalan

An open door may tempt a saint.   — English

He that labours is tempted by one devil; he that is

idle is tempted by a thousand.   — English

All temptations are found either in hope or fear.
                                        — English

Who avoids temptation avoids sin.   — American

Constant occupation prevents temptation.
                                        — American

Thrift

You will lack nothing if you think privation is
always with you.
Fujiyu wo tsune to omoeba fusoku nashi.
                                        — Japanese

One coin saved, a hundred losses.
Ichi-mon oshimi no hyaku-zon.   — Japanese

Thrift is a great revenue.   — English

A little, often, leaves wrinkles in the purse.

An beagan, go minic, a ghagas roic sa sparan.

                                              — Irish

Abundance maketh poor.   — English

No alchemy like savings.   — English

Tolerance

A man who lets his problems get the better of him
is like a man who divorces his wife the first time
she makes him angry.   — Malagasy

If you beat even new floor mats, dirt will
come out.

Atarashii tatami demo tatakeba gomi ga deru.

— Japanese

Even monkeys fall from trees.
Saru mo ki kara ochiru.   — Japanese

A faultless person has seven faults, a faulty person
forty-eight faults.
Nakute nana kuse, atte shijuhachi kuse.

— Japanese

The stumbling of a fabulous horse.
Ryume no tsumazuki.   — Japanese

The base of a lighthouse is dark.
Todai moto kurashi.   — Japanese

Tradition

Old used-to-do-it-this-way don't help none today.
— African American

Tradition must be a springboard to the future, not an easy chair for resting.

Hamesoret tzreecha lihiyot keresh k'feetza le'ateed v'lo kursa lish'at m'nucha. — Hebrew

The tree remains, but not so the hand that put it.

Maireann an crann, ach ni mhaireann an lamh a chuir e. — Irish

Trust

To know one's self is to know others, for heart can understand heart. — Chinese

When there is trust, no proof is necessary. When there is none, no proof is possible. — Chinese

Ask no favors and people everywhere are affable; if you don't drink, it doesn't matter what price wine is. — Chinese

If you suspect someone, don't employ them; if you employ someone, don't suspect them.

— Chinese

To trust is good; not to trust is better.
Fidarsi é bene, non fidarsi é meglio. — Italian

A secret is between two; when a third is involved, it's no secret.
Hasod bain shneiyeem; v'sod hashlosha aino sod.

— Hebrew

Don't put your trust in princes, or the sons of men; there is no salvation in them.
Al tivt'chu bin'deeveem, b'ven adam she'ain lo t'shu'a.

— Hebrew

Women don't know what a secret is.
Ain sod b'nasheem. — Hebrew

It's easy to trust a cat once you put the cream out of reach. — Mexican

He loses his thanks who promises and delays. — Mexican

He who covers you discovers you. — Mexican

A secret between two is God's secret; a secret between three is known to all. — Mexican

He who keeps a secret prevents much mischief. — Mexican

Few are fit to be entrusted with themselves. — English

Love many, trust few. — American

If you trust before you try, you may repent before
you die.   — English

You'll beguile none but those that trust you.
                                            — English

Trust not a new friend or an old enemy.
                                            — English

Trust God and keep your powder dry.
                                            — English

Never trust a man who doesn't trust others.
                                            — American

Truth

Dog don't get mad when you say he's a dog.
                                            — African American

The way of this world is to praise dead saints and persecute living ones.   — Dominican Republic

The truth is bitter and lies are sweet.
La verdad amarga y la mentira es dulce.
— Honduran

Do not bear ill will toward those who tell you the truth.
No quieras mal a quien te dice la verdad.
— Guatemalan

From the mouths of babes and drunkards, you will learn the truth.
Mipee katan v'shikor nitan l'galot et ha'emet.
— Japanese

To tell only half the truth is to give life to a new lie.   — Chinese

Concealing truth is like wearing embroidered
clothes and traveling by night.   — Chinese

Truth suffers but never perishes.
La verdad padece pero no perece.   — Mexican

False hope kills more readily than bitter truth.
Mata más una esperanza que un desengaño.
                                                        — Mexican

Truth comes back where she has once visited.
                                                        — English

Fools and children tell the truth.   — English

Half the truth is often a whole lie.   — English

Folks like the truth that hits their neighbor.

— American

Conscience is only another name for truth.

— American

Value

An eye is small but its usefulness is great.

— Mamprussi

When you go to fetch water and do not return, they do not inquire about the pot.   — Oji

The costliest clock can show only sixty minutes in every hour.

Der teirster zaiguer ken nit veizen mer vee zechtzig minit in yeden shtundeh.   — Hebrew

The milk of black goats and white goats is all
the same.
*Chalav eezeem sh'chorot v'chalav eezeem l'vanot
echad hu.* — Hebrew

The rainbow might be better lookin' if 'twasn't
such a cheap show. — African American

Something well cared for lasts two centuries.
— Russian

Chipped china lasts two centuries. — Russian

A handful of dirt is pleasing if it's your own land.
— Russian

What costs little is little esteemed. — English

What is gold is worth gold. — English

Don't value a gem by what it is set in.

— American

Vanity

No matter how beautiful the shoes are, they still have to go on the ground. — Haitian

Them short fe singer when dem put peacock in a choir. — Jamaican

Acorns compare their height with each other.
Donguri no sei kurabe. — Japanese

Kyoto people ruin themselves for clothing, Osaka people for food.
Kyo no kidaore, Osaka no kuidaore. — Japanese

The marten is proud where there is no weasel.
Itachi naki ma no ten hokori. — Japanese

Please the eye and plague the heart. — English

We are often shot with our own feathers.
— English

Vision

If we blink the eyes in order not to see a wicked person, how shall we be able to see a good person?
— Xhosa

Everything in the past died yesterday; everything in the future was born today. — Chinese

Weaving a net is better than praying for fish at the edge of the water. — Chinese

Remember to dig the well long before you get thirsty. — Chinese

Whether we walk quickly or slowly, the road remains the same. — Chinese

An overturned cart ahead warns the one behind. — Chinese

He who asks a question does not err easily. — Mexican

Love makes a good eye squint. — English

What is extraordinary, try to look at with your own eyes. — English

Faith is the vision of the heart.   — American

Vulnerability

The spot that makes the warrior Benkei cry.
Benkei no naki-dokoro.   — Japanese

A bee stinging a crying face.
Nakittsura ni hachi.   — Japanese

Want

Nothing can suffice a person except that which
they have not.   — African American

What you deserve you don't have to ask for.
          — Haitian

He that gets forgets, but he that wants thinks on.
          — English

Want is the whetstone of wit. — English

Wealth/Poverty

"What shall I add for the poor?" asked God.
"Fingernails and itch," answered the poor.

— Oromo

If you don't want to resign yourself to poverty,
resign yourself to work. — Hausan

The idle remarks of the rich are taken as maxims
of wisdom by the poor. — Ecuadoran

Poverty does not destroy virtue nor wealth
bestow it. — Colombian

For the lazy and the poor, everything always takes
twice the effort. — Honduran

Charity is not a bone you throw to a dog, but a
bone you share with a dog.   — Chinese

Great wealth is a gift from heaven; moderate
wealth results from frugality.   — Chinese

Wealth and obscurity cannot equal poverty
and fame.   — Chinese

Burn one day's gathering of firewood on the
same day.   — Chinese

One courts misfortune by flaunting wealth.
                                      — Chinese

The greatest charity is to enable the poor to earn
a living.   — Hebrew

Poverty is no disgrace, but neither do you have to take pride in it.
Orimkeit iz nit kein beesha, ober darfst nit shtoltzirin mit im. — Hebrew

Whoever hastens to grow rich will not go unpunished.
Arz l'ha'asheer lo yinakeh. — Hebrew

A crook in the Forth is worth an Earldom in the North. — Scottish

Hae you gear, or hae you nane, tine heart and a' is gone. — Scottish

Better saucht wi' little aucht than care wi' mony cows. — Scottish

Wealth consists not of having great possessions but of having few wants. — American

Weather

E'ening grey and a morning red, put on your hat or ye'll weet your head; e'ening red an' a morning grey is a taiken o' a bonny day. — Scottish

The men o' the East are pykin their geese, and sendin' their feathers here-awa there-awa.
— Scottish

When Falkland Hill puts on his cap, the Howe o' Fife will get a drap, and when the Bishop draws his cowl, look out for wind and weather fowl!
— Scottish

Snailie, snailie, shoot out yer horn, and tell us if it'll be a bonny day the morn. — Scottish

For a morning rain leave not your journey.

— English

A snow year, a rich year.　　　　　— English

Winter's thunder is summer's wonder.

— English

Fools are weatherwise, and those that are
weatherwise are seldom otherwise.　　— English

For every fog in March there's a frost in May.

— English

When you see the gossaner flying, be sure the air
is drying.　　　　　　　　　　— American

When the glow worm lights her lamp, the air is
always very damp.　　　　　　　— American

Warm weather in June sets the corn in tune.

— American

Wisdom

When the bait is more than the fish, 'tis time to stop fishing. — African American

Teach your descendants the two proper roads— literature and farming. — Chinese

Intelligence is endowed, but wisdom is learned.

— Chinese

Wisdom is attained by learning when to hold one's tongue. — Chinese

The merciful do not engage in war, and the righteous do not engage in finances.

— Chinese

He who knows he is a fool is not a big fool.

—— Chinese

Do not judge a person until the lid of his coffin
is closed. —— Chinese

Better to ride an ass that carries me than a horse
that throws me.
*Piuttosto un asino che porti, che un cavallo che butti
in terra.* —— Italian

What a fool does in the end, the wise man does in
the beginning.
Ció che lo stolto fa in fine, il savio fa in principio.
—— Italian

A wise man cares not for what he cannot have.
La gente savia non si cura di quei che non puo avere.
—— Italian

An evil act runs a thousand miles.
Akuji sen-ri o hashiru. — Japanese

By poking at a bamboo thicket, one drives out
a snake.
Yabu o tsutsuite hebi o dasu. — Japanese

Obey the customs of the village you enter.
Go ni itte wa go ni shitagae. — Japanese

The air of the Land of Israel makes one wise.
Aveera d'eretz yisrael machkeem. — Hebrew

Wisdom without morality is like a ring without
a gem.
Chochma blee mif'al k'etz blee pree. — Hebrew

The hearts of fools are in their mouths but the mouths of the wise are in their hearts.

B'fee k'seeleem libam u'v'lev chachameem peehem.

— Hebrew

While life yet lasts, laughter and molasses.

Mientras dura, vida y dulzura. — Mexican

Words and feathers are carried away by the wind.

— Mexican

The more one looks, the less one sees.

Quien más mira menos ve. — Mexican

Walk your own road and bear your own load.

Anda tu camino sin ayuda de vecino.

— Mexican

A wise man carries his cloak in fair weather, an' a fool wants his in rain. — Scottish

On painting and fighting look adreich. — Scottish

Ne'er misca' a Gordon in the raws o' Strathbogie. — Scottish

A wise man gets learning frae them that hae nane o' their ane. — Scottish

The Italians are wise before the deed; the Germans in the deed; the French after the deed. — English

The most manifest sign of wisdom is a continual cheerfulness. — English

The wind in one's face makes one wise.

— English

It takes great wisdom to play the fool.

— English

Wisdom doesn't always speak in Greek and Latin.

— American

Wit

A bean-jam rice cake into the open mouth.
Aita kuchi ni botamochi.

— Japanese

Like trying to put a comb upon the nun's head.
Bikuni ni kushi wo saseru yo.

— Japanese

Like a millstone dressed in a kimono.
Ishi-usu ni kimono wo kiseta yo.

— Japanese

The criticism of a blind man.
Mekura ni chochin. — Japanese

Use your wit as a shield, not as a sword.
— English

What is a man but his mind? — English

Brevity is the soul of wit. — American

If you have wit and learning, add to it wisdom
and modesty. — American

Women

Woman is like your shadow: follow her, she flies;
fly from her, she follows. — Argentinean

A woman's honor consists in the good opinion the
world has of her. — Cuban

A mother has little love for a son who did not give her pain. — Venezuelan

A bit but and a bit ben maks a mim maiden at the board end. — Scottish

A's no gowd that glitters, nor maidens that wear their hair. — Scottish

A crooning coo, a crawing hen, and a whistlin' maid were ne're very chancy. — Scottish

A worthy woman is the crown of her husband. — English

There is nothing better than a good woman and nothing worse than a bad one. — American

A woman can't drive her husband, but she can lead him. — American

Work

A crooked stick makes us know the carpenter.

— Oji

Sow when you dislike; you will reap when you like.

— Hausan

If the kernels are not finished, the jaw will not rest.
— Igbo

Those who labor with their minds rule; those who labor with their bodies are ruled.
— Chinese

If you have nothing to do, go home early.
— Chinese

Better to learn one thing well than to know ten superficially.
— Chinese

Do not gaze at the sky from the bottom of a well.
— Chinese

It is in our work that we discover love and faith.
— Mexican

Better a donkey that tarries than one that won't carry its load.
Más vale burro que arrear que no carga que cargar.
— Mexican

Everyone is the son of his own works.
— Mexican

The lazy work twice as much.
El flojo trabaja doble.
— Mexican

No one knows for whom they work.

Nadie sabe para quién trabaja.   — Mexican

Changes o' wark is a lightening o' hearts.
                                        — Scottish

I'm forejidged, forefoughten, and forejeskit.
                                        — Scottish

All work and no play make Jack a dull boy.
                                        — English

It is not work that kills, but worry.   — English

The devil finds work for idle hands.   — English

Many hands make light work.   — English

Hell is full of good meanings, but heaven is full of
good works.   — American

Bibliography

Beckwith, Martha. *Jamaica Proverbs.*
New York: Negro Universities Press, 1970.

Bitar, Farid, ed. *Treasury of Arabic Love: Poems,
Quotations and Proverbs in Arabic and
English.* New York: Hippocrene Books,
1996.

Branyon, Richard A., ed. *Treasury of Italian Love
Poems, Quotations and Proverbs.* New York:
Hippocrene Books, 1995.

Bryan, Ashley. *The Night Has Ears.* New York:
Atheneum Books for Young Readers, 1999.

Buchanan, Daniel Crump. *Japanese Proverbs
and Sayings.* Norman: University of
Oklahoma Press, 1965.

Champion, Selwyn Gurney. *Racial Proverbs: A Selection of the World's Proverbs Arranged Linguistically.* New York: Macmillan Publishing, 1938.

Collis, Harry. *101 American English Proverbs: Understanding Language and Culture Through Commonly Used Sayings.* Chicago: NTC Publishing Group, 1992.

Fitzhenry, Robert I. *The Harper Book of Quotations.* 3rd edition. New York: HarperCollins, 1993.

Galef, David. *"Even Monkeys Fall From Trees" and other Japanese Proverbs.* Tokyo: Charles E. Tuttle Co., 1997.

Gross, David C., ed. *Dictionary of 1000 Jewish Proverbs.* New York: Hippocrene Books, 1997.

Gross, David C., and Esther R. Gross, eds. *Jewish Wisdom: A Treasury of Proverbs, Maxims, Aphorisms, Wise Sayings and Memorable Quotations.* New York: Fawcett Crest, 1992.

Habibian, Simin K., ed. *1001 Persian-English Proverbs.* Bethesda, Maryland: Ibex Publishers, 1999.

Ibekwe, Patrick. *Wit and Wisdom of Africa: Proverbs from Africa and the Caribbean.* Trenton, New Jersey: Africa World Press, 1998.

Lau, Theodora. *Best-Loved Chinese Proverbs.* New York: HarperPerennial, 1995.

Lin, Marjorie, and Leonard Shalk, eds. *Dictionary of 1000 Chinese Proverbs.* New York: Hippocrene Books, 1998.

Mertvago, Peter, ed. *Dictionary of 1000 Italian Proverbs.* New York: Hippocrene Books, 1997.

Mertvago, Peter, ed. *Dictionary of 1000 Russian Proverbs.* New York: Hippocrene Books, 1998.

Mieder, Wolfgang, Stewart A. Kingsbury, and Kelsie B. Harder, eds. *A Dictionary of American Proverbs.* New York: Oxford University Press, 1992.

O'Donnell, James. *Classic Irish Proverbs.* In Ireland—Belfast: Appletree Press, 1997. In U.S.—San Francisco: Chronicle Books, 1998.

Pickering, David. *Cassell Dictionary of Proverbs.* London, England: Cassell, 1997.

Quesada, Roberto. *"When the Road Is Long, Even Slippers Feel Tight": A Collection of Latin American Proverbs.* Kansas City: Andrews McMeel Publishing, 1998.

Scottish Proverbs. New York: Hippocrene Books, 1998.

Sellers, Jeff M. *Folk Wisdom of Mexico.* San Francisco: Chronicle Books, 1994.

Walker, Colin S. K. *Scottish Proverbs.* New York: Barnes and Noble, 1996.

Whiting, Bartlett Jere. *Modern Proverbs and Proverbial Sayings.* Cambridge, Mass. and London, England: Harvard University Press, 1989.

Williams, Fionnuala Carson. *Irish Proverbs*. New York: Sterling Publishing Co., Inc., 2000.

Zona, Guy A. *"Eyes That See Do Not Grow Old": The Proverbs of Mexico, Central and South America*. New York: Touchstone, 1996.

Zona, Guy A. *"If You Have Two Loaves of Bread, Sell One And Buy A Lily" And Other Proverbs Of China*. New York: Touchstone, 1997.

Zona, Guy A. *"The Soul Would Have No Rainbow If The Eyes Had No Tears" and Other Native American Proverbs*. New York: Touchstone, 1994.

Index

A

F

O

P

507

T

U

V

If you liked this book, you'll love this series:

Giant Encyclopedia of Aromatherapy • Little Giant Encyclopedia of Baseball Quizzes • Little Giant Encyclopedia of Card & Magic Tricks • Little Giant Encyclopedia of Card Games • Little Giant Encyclopedia of Card Games Gift Set • Little Giant Encyclopedia of Dream Symbols • Little Giant Encyclopedia of Fortune Telling • Little Giant Encyclopedia of Gambling Games • Little Giant Encyclopedia of Games for One or Two • Little Giant Encyclopedia of Handwriting Analysis • Little Giant Encyclopedia of Home Remedies • Little Giant Encyclopedia of IQ Tests • Little Giant Encyclopedia of Logic Puzzles • Little Giant Encyclopedia of Magic • Little Giant Encyclopedia of Mazes • Little Giant Encyclopedia of Meditations & Blessings • Little Giant Encyclopedia of Mensa Mind-Teasers • Little Giant Encyclopedia of Names • Little Giant Encyclopedia of Natural Healing • Little Giant Encyclopedia of One-Liners • Little Giant Encyclopedia of Palmistry • Little Giant Encyclopedia of Proverbs • Little Giant Encyclopedia of Puzzles • Little Giant Encyclopedia of Runes • Little Giant Encyclopedia of Spells & Magic • Little Giant Encyclopedia of Superstitions • Little Giant Encyclopedia of Toasts & Quotes • Little Giant Encyclopedia of Travel & Holiday Games • Little Giant Encyclopedia of UFOs • Little Giant Encyclopedia of Wedding Toasts • Little Giant Encyclopedia of Word Puzzles • Little Giant Encyclopedia of the Zodiac

Available at fine stores everywhere.